interchange

Jack C. Richards
Revised by John Chapman

3

VIDEO RESOURCE BOOK

CAMBRIDGE
UNIVERSITY PRESS

CAMBRIDGE UNIVERSITY PRESS
Cambridge, New York, Melbourne, Madrid, Cape Town,
Singapore, São Paulo, Delhi, Tokyo, Mexico City

Cambridge University Press
32 Avenue of the Americas, New York, NY 10013-2473, USA

www.cambridge.org
Information on this title: www.cambridge.org/9781107636934

First published 2012

Printed in the United States of America

A catalog record for this publication is available from the British Library.

ISBN 978-1-107-65708-3 Intro DVD
ISBN 978-1-107-69753-9 Intro Video Resource Book
ISBN 978-1-107-62524-2 DVD 1
ISBN 978-1-107-64367-3 Video Resource Book 1
ISBN 978-1-107-66521-7 DVD 2
ISBN 978-1-107-65180-7 Video Resource Book 2
ISBN 978-1-107-62067-4 DVD 3
ISBN 978-1-107-63693-4 Video Resource Book 3

Art direction, book design, photo research, and layout services: Integra

Contents

■ **Plan of Video 3**   v

■ **Introduction**   vi

   Interchange Video Program   vi

   Video in the classroom   vi

   Program length   vi

   Program components   vi

   Guidelines for teaching the *Interchange* Video Program   vi

   How to teach a typical video sequence   vii

1 Dream Date   2

2 Career moves   6

3 Common ground   10

4 Around the campfire   14

5 Travel World   18

6 What's the problem?   22

7 Endangered islands   26

8 Tango!   30

9 Stressed out   34

10 The Virtual Office   38

11 Live and learn   42

12 Good business   46

13 Stonehenge   50

14 Making music   54

15 The streets of Montreal   58

16 The Harlem Children's Zone   62

■ **Teaching notes**   66

■ **Video transcripts**   116

Credits

Illustration credits

Andrezzinho: 7, 22; Ralph Butler: 17, 40; Paul Daviz: 6, 18 (*top*), 42; Carlos Diaz: 12, 36; Chuck Gonzales: 5, 14 (*top*), 35, 45; Jim Haynes: 2, 34;

Trevor Keen: 14 (*bottom*), 44; KJA-artists.com: 4, 54; Robert Schuster: 18 (*bottom*), 56; James Yamasaki: 8, 16, 24

Photography credits

2 ©Fuse/Getty Images; 10 ©Mary Kate Denny/PhotoEdit; 21 ©Monkey Business Images/Shutterstock; 22 ©Steve Dunwell/Ticket/Photolibrary; 25 ©kak2s/Shutterstock; 26 (*top*) ©Peter Harrison/Ticket/Photolibrary; (*bottom*) ©U.S. Coast Guard/Science Faction/SuperStock; 30 (*top*) ©Adalberto Ríos Szalay/Age Fotostock; (*bottom*) ©Comstock Images/Getty Images; 32 (*notebook*) ©Igor A. Bondarenko/Shutterstock; (*clockwise from top left*) ©IMAGEMORE Co., Ltd./Getty Images; ©Nick White/Digital Vision/Getty Images; ©Masterfile; ©Tim Robberts/Riser/Getty Images; 33 ©Erik Isakson/Tetra Images/Corbis;

34 ©forestpath/Shutterstock; 38 (*top row, left to right*) ©06photo/Shutterstock; ©Mixa/Age Fotostock; ©Masterfile; (*bottom row, left to right*) ©David M. Grossman/The Image Works; ©Yuri Arcurs/Shutterstock; 46 ©Lonely Planet/SuperStock; 50 ©Marcia Chambers/dbimages/Alamy; 51 (*center right and right*) ©Adam Stanford/Aerial-Cam Photography; 52 (*left to right*) ©Scherl/SZ Photo/The Image Works; ©Nataiki/Shutterstock; 54 ©Collage Photography/Veer; 58 ©Spencer Platt/Getty Images; 60 ©Brigette Sullivan/PhotoEdit; ©David Grossman/Alamy

Video credits

Unit 7 ©BBC Worldwide Americas Inc. Used with permission. Unit 10 ©ABC News. Used with permission. Footage from The Crayon Marketing Firm used with permission.

Unit 13 ©A&E Television Networks. All rights reserved. Used with permission. Unit 16 courtesy of *60 Minutes*. ©Copyright CBS News. Used with permission.

Plan of Video 3

1 Dream Date A young woman chooses one of three men for her date on a dating game show.

Functional Focus Expressing feelings; describing personalities
Grammar Clauses containing *it* with adverbial clauses
Vocabulary Adjectives to describe personalities

2 Career moves A career advisor talks about the importance of someone's personality type in choosing a major and profession.

Functional Focus Describing personality types
Grammar Gerunds as subjects and objects
Vocabulary Words related to jobs and personality types

3 Common ground A woman asks her friend to look after her younger sister overnight.

Functional Focus Asking favors
Grammar Indirect requests
Vocabulary Requests and responses

4 Around the campfire Three friends on a camping trip share a spooky story and meet a mysterious stranger.

Functional Focus Telling a story in the past
Grammar Past tense verbs: past continuous, simple past, past perfect
Vocabulary Unusual events

5 Travel World Reporters around the world ask people about cross-cultural experiences.

Functional Focus Describing customs
Grammar Expectations: (*not*) *expected to*, (*not*) *supposed to*, (*not*) *customary to*, (*not*) *acceptable to*
Vocabulary Words related to traveling abroad

6 What's the problem? A couple's hope for a relaxing weekend at a quaint hotel is dashed.

Functional Focus Describing problems; making complaints
Grammar *Need* with passive infinitives and gerunds
Vocabulary Words to describe problems

7 Endangered islands A BBC reporter explains how climate change threatens the island nation of Tuvalu.

Functional Focus Describing environmental problems
Grammar The passive and prepositions of cause
Vocabulary Words related to the environment and climate change

8 Tango! A reporter talks to several people about learning to dance the tango.

Functional Focus Talking about learning methods
Grammar Gerunds and infinitives; *would rather* and *would prefer*
Vocabulary Words related to learning

9 Stressed out A woman seeks advice from a co-worker on how to relieve stress.

Functional Focus Making suggestions
Grammar Making suggestions with gerunds, infinitives, base-form verbs, and negative questions
Vocabulary Idioms related to stress

10 The Virtual Office ABC News presents a report on the changing face of the workplace.

Functional Focus Comparing old and new ways of doing things
Grammar Predicting the future with *will*
Vocabulary Terms to describe the modern office

11 Live and learn A host asks people to share embarrassing stories.

Functional Focus Talking about past mistakes
Grammar *Should have/shouldn't have* + past participle; *if* clauses + past perfect
Vocabulary Words to describe embarrassment

12 Good business A student interviews a local business owner about her secrets of success.

Functional Focus Discussing what makes a business successful
Grammar Infinitive clauses and phrases of purpose
Vocabulary Words to describe a café

13 Stonehenge The History Channel presents current scientific theories on the mysterious origin and purpose of Stonehenge.

Functional Focus Explaining past events
Grammar Past modals for degrees of certainty
Vocabulary Words to describe an ancient civilization

14 Making music A look at how a song is written, is produced, and gets played on the air.

Functional Focus Describing the steps in a process
Grammar The passive to describe process
Vocabulary Words related to music production

15 The streets of Montreal A reporter in Montreal, Quebec, Canada, interviews people about bicycling in the city.

Functional Focus Expressing opinions about city rules
Grammar Passive modals
Vocabulary Words related to traffic and safety

16 The Harlem Children's Zone An interview with Geoffrey Canada, an education reformer in the U.S., excerpted from the CBS News program *60 Minutes*.

Functional Focus Talking about challenges
Grammar Complex noun phrases with gerunds
Vocabulary Words related to education

Introduction

■ *INTERCHANGE* VIDEO PROGRAM

The philosophy underlying *Interchange* is that learning a second or foreign language is more meaningful and effective when the language is used for real communication instead of being studied as an end in itself. The *Interchange* Video Program brings this philosophy to life by providing a variety of entertaining and instructive live-action video sequences ("videos") along with a wealth of activities that reinforce and extend the content of the videos. The program serves as an exciting vehicle for introducing and practicing useful conversational language for everyday situations.

The *Interchange* Video Program is designed to complement the Student's Books. Each video provides further practice related to the topics, language, and vocabulary introduced in the corresponding unit of the Student's Book.

■ VIDEO IN THE CLASSROOM

The use of video in the classroom can be an exciting and effective way to teach and learn. As a medium, video both motivates and entertains students. The *Interchange* Video Program is a unique resource that does the following:

- Depicts dynamic, natural contexts for language use.
- Uses engaging story lines to present authentic language as well as cultural information about speakers of English.
- Enables learners to use visual information to enhance comprehension.
- Focuses on the important cultural dimension of learning a language by actually showing how speakers of the language live and behave.
- Allows learners to observe the gestures, facial expressions, and other aspects of body language that accompany speech.

Learners can expand their cultural awareness, develop skills and strategies for communicating effectively, and learn to use language creatively.

■ PROGRAM LENGTH

There are sixteen videos in each level of the *Interchange* Video Program, one video for every Student's Book unit. For Level 3, they vary slightly in length, but in general, each video is three to five minutes long.

The accompanying material in the Video Resource Book is designed for maximum flexibility and provides 45 to 90 minutes of classroom activity.

■ PROGRAM COMPONENTS

Video

The sixteen videos in each level's video program complement Units 1 through 16 of the corresponding Student's Book. For Level 3, there are six dramatized stories and ten documentary-style sequences. Although linked to the topic of the corresponding Student's Book unit, the videos present new situations and introduce characters who do not appear in the text. The language used in the videos reflects the structures and vocabulary presented in the Student's Book, while also illustrating how language is used by English speakers in a variety of situations.

Video Resource Book

The Video Resource Book contains photocopiable worksheets for students, detailed teaching notes with worksheet answer keys, and complete video transcripts. The worksheets and teaching notes correspond to each video in the program and are organized into four sections: *Preview, Watch the video, Follow-up*, and *Language close-up*.

■ GUIDELINES FOR TEACHING THE *INTERCHANGE* VIDEO PROGRAM

The *Interchange* Video Program provides a multi-skills language learning experience in which each element builds on and supports the others.

The *Preview* activities build on each other to provide students with relevant background information and key vocabulary that will assist them in better understanding the video. The carefully sequenced *Watch the video* activities first help students focus on gist and then guide them in identifying important details and language. These tasks also prepare them for *Follow-up* speaking activities, which encourage students to extend and personalize information by voicing their opinions or carrying out communicative tasks. Then students finish with the *Language close-up*, examining and practicing the particular language structures and functions presented in the video.

▓ HOW TO TEACH A TYPICAL VIDEO SEQUENCE

The unit-by-unit teaching notes in the Video Resource Book give detailed suggestions for teaching each unit. In addition to these comprehensive notes, here is a set of procedures that can be used to teach any of the units of the *Interchange* Video Program.

First, introduce the topic of the unit by asking questions and eliciting information from the students related to the theme of the unit. Explain what they will study (e.g., main topics, functions, and structures) and give students an indication of what they will see in the video. Present the activities and tasks using the following guidelines:

Preview

Culture These activities introduce the topics of the video sequences and provide important background and cultural information.

- Introduce the topic by asking questions about it.
- Have students read the culture note silently.
- Answer any questions about vocabulary or content.
- Read the questions aloud. Then have students work in pairs or small groups to answer them.
- Discuss students' answers.

Vocabulary These activities introduce and practice the essential vocabulary of the videos through a variety of interesting tasks.

- Introduce and model the pronunciation of the words in the activity.
- Have students complete the task in pairs or individually.
- Have students compare answers with a partner or around the class.
- Check students' answers.
- Encourage students to supply additional related vocabulary items where appropriate.

Guess the facts/Guess the story These activities allow students to make predictions about characters and their actions by watching part of the video, by watching all of the video with the sound off, by looking at photos in the worksheets, or by activating personal knowledge of the topic through discussion questions. These schema-building activities improve

students' comprehension when they watch the full video with sound.

- Ask students to guess what the video is about by thinking about the topic of the unit and looking at the photos. Accept all answers at this stage.
- Explain the task and lead students through the procedure. Answer any questions that arise.
- Play the video as instructed for that unit.
- Have students complete the task individually or in pairs.
- Have students check their predictions and compare answers with a partner or around the class.
- Check students' answers, replaying portions of the video as appropriate.

Watch the video

Get the picture These initial viewing activities help students gain a global understanding of the videos by focusing on gist. Activity types vary from unit to unit, but typically involve watching for key information needed to complete a chart, answer questions, or arrange events in sequential order.

- Direct students' attention to the task, and read through it with them. Answer vocabulary or procedural questions as they arise.
- Have individual students predict answers to questions if they feel they have enough information to do so.
- Remind students that this is a gist activity. They don't need to understand every detail in the video.
- Play the entire video with the sound on. Replay if necessary.
- Have students complete the task individually or in pairs. When appropriate, have them check the predictions they made in previewing activities.
- Have students compare answers with a partner or around the class.
- If time permits, have students check answers while watching the video again.
- Check students' answers.

Watch for details Students focus on more detailed meaning by watching and listening for specific information to complete the tasks.

- Explain the task. Lead students through the instructions and questions.
- Answer any vocabulary and procedural questions that arise.
- Play the entire video with the sound on. Replay as necessary.

- Have students complete the task individually or in pairs.
- Have students compare answers with a partner or around the class.
- If time permits, have students check their answers while watching the video again.
- Check students' answers.

What's your opinion? Students make inferences about the characters' actions, feelings, and motivations, or state their own opinions about topics in the video.

Follow-up

Role play, interview, and other expansion activities This section includes communicative activities based on the videos in which students extend and personalize what they have learned. Encourage students to use new language to talk about themselves and their ideas as they complete the tasks.

- Explain the task. Lead students through the procedure and answer their vocabulary and procedural questions.
- Have students complete the task individually, in pairs, or in small groups, as noted in the teaching notes.
- Have students compare answers in pairs or in small groups.
- When appropriate, have volunteer pairs or groups act out the activity for the class.

Language close-up

What did they say? These cloze activities develop bottom-up listening skills by having students focus on the specific language in the videos and then fill in missing words.

- Lead students through the task instructions. Answer procedural questions as necessary.
- Have students read the cloze passage and predict answers when possible.
- Play the appropriate section of the video and do a spot-check to gauge overall comprehension. Do not supply answers at this stage.
- Play the section again. Have students compare answers with a partner or around the class. Replay as necessary.
- Go over answers with the class, and discuss any trouble spots.
- If you wish, divide the class in half or in groups and lead a choral repetition and practice of the cloze passage. When students are comfortable with

it, have them practice it in pairs or small groups, depending on the number of characters required.
- Have selected pairs or groups read or act out the passage for the class.

Grammar and functional activities In these activities, which are titled to reflect the structural and functional focus of a particular unit, students practice the grammatical structures and functions presented in the videos. These activities vary from unit to unit, but teachers can follow these procedures generally:

- Present the grammatical structure and give example sentences from the video script or from students' experiences.
- Lead students through the task and answer vocabulary and procedural questions as needed.
- Have students complete the task individually or in pairs.
- Have students compare answers with a partner or around the class.
- Check students' answers.
- Review the grammatical structure as appropriate.
- Refer students back to the Grammar Focus in the appropriate unit of Student's Book 3 as necessary.

Options for the classroom

The richness of video as a learning medium provides teachers with many options for the classroom. The Video Resource Book provides step-by-step instructions for all of the activities in the photocopiable worksheets; however, teachers should not feel restricted by these instructions. Once teachers feel comfortable with the basic course procedures, they can try other effective – and enjoyable – classroom techniques for presenting and working with the videos. Teachers are also encouraged to use the videos as springboards for further classroom activities appropriate to their teaching and learning situations. Here are several proven techniques.

Fast-forward viewing For activities in which students watch the video with the sound off, play the entire sequence on fast-forward and have students list all of the things they see. For example, for *Unit 5: Travel World*, have students watch the sequence in fast-forward and list all of the countries they see. Nearly all of the activities designed to be completed with the sound off can be done in this manner.

Information gap Play approximately the first half of a video, and then have students work in pairs or groups to predict what will happen next. For example, in *Unit 3: Common ground*, stop the video just after Anne leaves her little sister, Megan, with Rachel. Ask students, "What do you think Megan and Rachel will do tonight?" Have students predict the answer, and then play the rest of the sequence so that students can check their predictions.

Act it out All of the videos provide an excellent basis for role plays and drama activities. Select a short scene, and have students watch it several times. Then have pairs or groups act out the scene, staying as close as possible to the actions and expressions of the characters. Have pairs or groups act out their scenes in front of the class.

Slow viewing Play a video in slow motion. As they view, have students call out all of the things people are doing, wearing, or eating – whatever is appropriate to a particular unit.

What are they saying? Have students watch a short segment of a video in which two people are talking, but without sound. Then have pairs use the context to predict what the people might be saying to each other. Have pairs write out sample dialogs and share their work with the class.

Freeze-frame Freeze a frame of a video and have students call out information about the scene: the objects they can see, what the people are doing, the time and place – whatever is appropriate to the scene or the learning situation.

Dream Date

1 CULTURE

In North America, many people start dating in their teens and early twenties. They meet at school or work, or they're introduced by friends. On dates, they go out in couples or in groups to movies, sporting events, and meals. Traditionally, the man paid for the date, but modern couples may decide to split the bill or let the person who made the invitation pay for both people.

How do people in your country meet each other? What do friends or dating couples like to do together? Where are some popular places to go? When a man and a woman (or a group of friends) go out together, who pays?

2 VOCABULARY *Personality types*

PAIR WORK How would you describe the people below? Choose a description from the box.

a good conversationalist	easygoing	generous
ambitious	✓ egotistical	straightforward

1. Jill is always talking about herself. She thinks she's better than other people.
   A: I think she's *egotistical*.
   B: Yes, I agree.
2. Mike is very relaxed. Nothing seems to upset him.
3. Paul always tells people exactly what he thinks. He doesn't hide his feelings.
4. Erika has big plans and works hard to achieve them.
5. John asks a lot of questions, and he's interested in what I have to say.
6. Leah is a great friend. She gives others a lot of her time and energy, and she also forgives others easily.

3 GUESS THE STORY

Elizabeth is going to choose one of these men to be her date. How do you think she will decide? Who will she choose?

Bachelor 1

Bachelor 2

Bachelor 3

4 GET THE PICTURE

A Look at your answers to Exercise 3. Did you guess correctly?

B Check (✓) the things Elizabeth said to the bachelors. Then compare with a partner.

- Describe to me your ideal date.
- How old are you?
- What's your favorite sport?
- Tell me two things about yourself: one positive and one negative.
- Finish this sentence: "I think it's disgusting when . . . "
- Finish this sentence: "My ideal date has . . . "

C What words describe Elizabeth and the bachelors? Write the correct word under each picture. Then compare with a partner.

| easygoing | egotistical | excited | straightforward |

5 WATCH FOR DETAILS

Correct the mistakes below. Then compare with a partner.

Bachelor 1 is a ~~reporter~~ _{writer} and a former college soccer coach who loves playing or watching almost

every kind of game. Bachelor 2 is a model, who also studies languages. Everyone should recognize

him from his latest jeans ad on buses and in magazines. Bachelor 3 is the Director of Educational

Programs at a high school. In his free time, he enjoys swimming, running, and dancing. He and

Elizabeth went to college together.

6 WHO SAID WHAT?

Who said the sentences below? Check (✓) the correct answers. Then compare with a partner.

	Bachelor 1	Bachelor 2	Bachelor 3
1. I'd be too embarrassed to tell you the truth.	☐	☐	☐
2. It really bothers me when people lie.	☐	☐	☐
3. It's hard to split my time among so many people!	☐	☐	☐
4. I'd take you out to a nice dinner.	☐	☐	☐
5. I think I'm a pretty good friend, and reliable.	☐	☐	☐
6. Actually, I'm a pretty good guy.	☐	☐	☐
7. Well, I'm pretty easygoing.	☐	☐	☐

Follow-up

7 ROLE PLAY Let's play Dream Date!

A **PAIR WORK** Imagine you are Elizabeth. Add two more questions to ask the bachelors.

1. Describe to me your ideal date.

2. Tell me two things about yourself: one positive and one negative.

3. Finish this sentence: "I can't stand it when . . . "

4. ....

5. ....

B **GROUP WORK** Now join another pair. Three of you are bachelors. The fourth person is Elizabeth.

Elizabeth: Take turns asking the three bachelors your questions. Then choose your dream date.

Bachelors: Answer Elizabeth's questions. Try to get Elizabeth to choose you as her dream date.

Interchange VRB 3 © Cambridge University Press 2012   Photocopiable

Language close-up

8 WHAT DID THEY SAY?

Watch the video and complete the conversation. Then practice it.

Elizabeth is asking the bachelors to complete a few sentences.

Elizabeth: Bachelor Number 1, finish this sentence:

"I .... it when . . ."

Bachelor 1: I .... it when . . . people

.... when I'm ....

.... the soccer match on TV.

Elizabeth: Bachelor Number 3, finish this sentence:

"I .... it's .... when . . ."

Bachelor 3: I .... it's .... when . . .

when I go to a fancy .... and I don't get

the .... I deserve.

Elizabeth: Bachelor Number 2, finish this sentence: "It .... me when . . . "

Bachelor 2: It .... me when . . . people .... over unimportant

things. I just think people should be less .... and more ....

9 CLAUSES CONTAINING IT WITH ADVERBIAL CLAUSES

A Complete the sentences about dates or friendships with phrases from the box. Then add two more statements of your own.

1. I can't stand it *when my date arrives late* ....

2. It makes me happy ....

3. I like it ....

4. It bothers me ....

5. It really upsets me ....

6. It embarrasses me ....

7. ....

8. ....

> ✓ arrive late
> forget to call me
> lie to me
> make me feel special
> send me flowers
> talk during a movie

B **PAIR WORK** Compare your statements with a partner. Which of your partner's statements are true for you?

2 Career moves

1 CULTURE

Choosing a career can be difficult if you're not sure what job is best for you. Experts suggest the following to help you make a decision:
- Take a career assessment test to find out what professions are a good match for you.
- Look at your educational and work achievements to determine your strengths and weaknesses.
- Think about your hobbies and free-time activities, and what they say about your interests, abilities, and values.
- Talk with a friend or family member who is a good listener, or consult with a career counselor.

Talk about your career plans. Which skills and abilities would you use in this future career? How is this type of work related to what you want to accomplish in life? How sure are you of your current career choice?

2 VOCABULARY *Attributes at work*

A Complete each sentence with a word from the box.

creative	collaborative	✓ independent	physical	practical	precise

1. My brother is very ...*independent*..... , so he prefers to work by himself.

2. My friend Elena is a graphic designer, which lets her use her imagination and be ....

3. My boss comes up with the big ideas, but I enjoy planning out the .... details.

4. Building a house requires .... strength and stamina.

5. The best part of working in a team is the .... process of making decisions together.

6. In finance, it's important to be .... and not make mistakes!

B **PAIR WORK** Describe yourself or someone you know well. Your partner describes the person's personality using one of the words from the box.

A: My friend makes a list of all the things he has to do each day.
B: He sounds like a practical person.

3 GUESS THE STORY

Watch the first minute of the video with the sound off.
Answer these questions.

1. Where is the conversation taking place?
2. Who do you think the man and woman are?
3. What do you think they are discussing?

Watch the video

4 GET THE PICTURE

A Look at your answers to Exercise 3. Did you guess correctly?

B What personality type did Ms. Auden think would be best suited to the jobs below?
Write the correct word under each picture. Then compare with a partner.

librarian	repair person	teacher	lawyer

5 MAKING INFERENCES

Which statements are probably true? Which are probably false?
Check (✓) your answers. Then compare with a partner.

	True	False
1. A conventional type would make a good actor.	☐	☐
2. Good waiters are often social types.	☐	☐
3. An enterprising type would not work for other people.	☐	☐
4. Most accountants are artistic types.	☐	☐
5. Someone who runs his or her own business is an investigative type.	☐	☐
6. Mechanics are often realistic types.	☐	☐
7. Studying animals in the wild would appeal to some investigative types.	☐	☐

6 WHAT'S YOUR OPINION?

A Read the description of each person's personality type below. Then write notes in the chart about which job at an advertising agency you think the person would enjoy, if any. Be sure to give reasons.

	Manager	Ad designer	Accountant
1. Bernie is a conventional type.	No: prefers to follow rules and procedures	No: doesn't enjoy creative things as much	Yes: likes details
2. Fatima is an enterprising type.			
3. Yoko is an investigative type.			
4. Carlos is an artistic type.			

B **GROUP WORK** Compare your answers with your group. Come up with one other job at the agency that would suit each person.

Follow-up

7 ARE THEY DOING THE RIGHT JOBS?

A Write the names of three people you know well. Tell what job each one does. Then describe each worker's personality type and explain why his or her job is right for them.

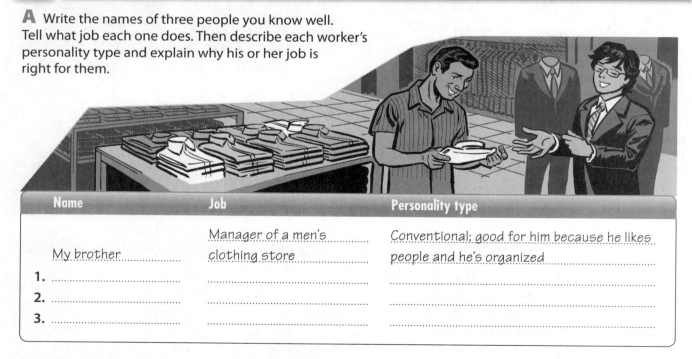

Name	Job	Personality type
My brother	Manager of a men's clothing store	Conventional; good for him because he likes people and he's organized
1.		
2.		
3.		

B **PAIR WORK** Take turns describing each person you wrote about to your partner. Answer any questions your partner may have.

8 WHAT DID THEY SAY?

Watch the video and complete the conversation. Then practice it.

Jacquelyn Auden talks with Jamie about personality types.

Ms. Auden: There are six .... personality types: .... ,
conventional, enterprising, investigative, realistic, and ....
The .... type is artistic. These .... are
.... and imaginative, and they .... to work
on one .... at a time, rather than multi-tasking.

Jamie: What .... should artistic .... pursue?

Ms. Auden: The most .... thing for .... type of people
is being in .... of a .... project. So,
.... to consider are landscaping, graphic .... , web design.

Jamie: I .... The .... personality type is conventional.
Tell us .... that one.

Ms. Auden: Yes. Conventional types are .... and orderly. They ....
well to rules, ... , schedules, ... like that.

9 GERUNDS AS SUBJECTS AND OBJECTS *Describing a job*

A Complete the sentences about a job using the gerund forms of the words and
phrases in the box. Then guess the job described.

encourage	organize the game schedule	work on weekends
improve their skills	stay in shape	✓ work with children

1. I enjoy ....working with children.... ; it helps me feel young.
2. .... is easy with all the running around
   I have to do.
3. I don't always enjoy .... ,
   but that's when our games are held.
4. At the end of the season, we have a big tournament, so I spend a lot of time
   .... for that event.
5. I help players concentrate on ....
6. .... weaker players helps the whole
   team improve.

Job described: ....

B **PAIR WORK** Choose a job and describe your duties. Can your partner guess
your job?

3 Common ground

1 CULTURE

Read this advice to babysitters in North America.

- Ask parents to show you the location of emergency exits, smoke detectors, and fire extinguishers.
- Make sure you have the telephone number of where the parents are going.
- If the children are up, know their location at all times and never leave them alone for too long. If the children are asleep, check on them about every fifteen minutes.
- Always get approval if you would like to have a visitor.
- In an emergency, call 911. Identify yourself by name, say you are babysitting, and state the problem. Say where you are and give the phone number you are calling from.

Is babysitting popular in your country? What would you enjoy about babysitting? What would be challenging? Write some suggestions or rules for babysitters to add to the list above.

2 VOCABULARY *Requests and responses*

PAIR WORK Match each request with a response. Then practice the requests and responses.

...d... 1. Is it all right if I use your phone?

.... 2. Would you mind my using your car?

.... 3. Is it OK if I drop her off?

.... 4. Could you ask her to bring something?

.... 5. I was wondering if you could help me out.

.... 6. Would you mind if she stayed with you?

a. No, go ahead. The keys are on the table.

b. OK. I'll tell her.

c. Sure. What can I do?

d. No, sorry. I'm expecting a call.

e. Not at all. I'd be happy to have her.

f. Sure. Or I can pick her up.

3 GUESS THE STORY

Watch the first minute of the video with the sound off.
What do you think the women are talking about?

4 GET THE PICTURE

First put the pictures in order (1 to 6). Then write the correct request under each picture. Compare with a partner.

Could you please turn down the volume?   Can we watch them?
Is it OK if I watch the movie now?   Would you mind if she stayed with you tonight?
Could I have something to eat?   Could we watch the second movie after this one is over?

....

....

....

....

5 MAKING INFERENCES

Which statements are probably true? Which are probably false?
Check (✓) your answers. Then compare with a partner.

	True	False
1. Anne is in a hurry.	☐	☐
2. Anne and Megan live together.	☐	☐
3. Rachel thinks it will be easy to get along with Megan.	☐	☐
4. Rachel is worried that Megan might interfere with her work.	☐	☐
5. Megan doesn't want to do her homework.	☐	☐
6. Megan doesn't care what food she eats.	☐	☐
7. Anne is surprised that Megan and Rachel became friends.	☐	☐

6 WHO SAID WHAT?

Who said the sentences below? Check (✓) the correct answers. Then compare with a partner.

	Anne	Rachel	Megan
1. I need a big favor.	☐	☐	☐
2. Hey, you've got the *Twilight* movies!	☐	☐	☐
3. How's the homework coming?	☐	☐	☐
4. I'm starving.	☐	☐	☐
5. You've never read any of the books or seen the movies?	☐	☐	☐
6. You two really seemed to hit it off.	☐	☐	☐

☰ Follow-up

7 ROLE PLAY

A PAIR WORK

Student A: You're planning a big party for this weekend. You want your friend (Student B) to help you. Write your requests in the box below. Then ask your friend for help.

Student B: Accept or decline your friend's (Student A's) requests.

1. I was wondering if I could borrow your vacuum cleaner.

2. ....

3. ....

A: I was wondering if I could borrow your vacuum cleaner.
B: Of course. Go right ahead!

B PAIR WORK

Student B: You're moving to a new apartment. You want your friend (Student A) to help you. Write your requests in the box below. Then ask your friend for help.

Student A: Accept or decline your friend's (Student B's) requests.

1. Is it OK if I borrow these boxes?

2. ....

3. ....

Language close-up

8 WHAT DID THEY SAY?

Watch the video and complete the conversation. Then practice it.

Anne asks her friend Rachel for a favor.

Anne: Rachel! I am so .... you're home. I was
.... if you could help me out.

Rachel: Yeah. .... , Anne?

Anne: I .... a big .... My ....
just called, and he wants me to go out of town ....
.... to meet with a client.

Rachel: ....

Anne: Yeah. But my .... are out of town, too, and my
little sister, Megan, is .... with me. ....
.... if she stayed with you
.... ? I .... pick her up .... by ten.

Rachel: No, I .... at all. What .... did you want to
.... her over?

Anne: How about .... ?

9 INDIRECT REQUESTS *Asking favors*

A Anne has asked Rachel to look after her apartment while she is away.
Anne has several requests for Rachel. Complete their phone conversation
with the correct form of the expressions in the box.

Anne: Would you mind <u>taking in the mail every day</u> ?

Rachel: Sure, no problem. I'll leave it on the table.

Anne: Great. And could you .... ?

Rachel: I'd love to. I've got some fish at home.

Anne: And let's see. I was wondering if you could
.... ?

Rachel: Sure. I'll water them once a day.

Anne: Great. Oh, and I was wondering if you'd mind
.... ?

Rachel: Yeah, I guess. How often does he need a walk?

Anne: Only three times a day. Anyway, one more thing. Is it OK if Megan
.... ?

Rachel: Are you kidding? Of course it's OK. Megan and I get along just fine.

| feed the fish |
| spend the weekend |
| ✓take in the mail every day |
| water the plants |
| walk the dog |

B **PAIR WORK** Imagine you are going away for a weekend, and your
partner is going to look after your apartment or house. Write several
requests. Then take turns asking each other the favors.

4 Around the campfire

1 *CULTURE*

North Americans enjoy telling stories, especially spooky stories about scary and mysterious things. Spooky stories are popular around the campfire, at sleepovers, and during the fall and winter months, especially near Halloween. People tell and listen to these stories as a way of dealing with their fear of the unknown. It's also fun to experience the thrill of fear while knowing that you're really safe.

Do you enjoy telling and listening to stories? Do you enjoy spooky or scary stories? Why or why not? Are stories about mysterious people and events popular in your culture? If you can, share a well-known story from your culture with some classmates.

2 *VOCABULARY* Descriptions

For each pair of pictures write the correct description.

1.

......surprised......

......freaked out......

freaked out
surprised

2.

....

....

a mysterious situation
a scary situation

3.

....

a scream
a hoot

4.

....

....

a farm
a campground

3 GUESS THE STORY

Check (✓) what you think is happening in each of the following situations.

- ☐ She has just taken a shower.
- ☐ She has just gone on a hike.

- ☐ She is going to make dinner.
- ☐ She is going to tell a story.

- ☐ He is greeting the girls.
- ☐ He is telling a spooky story.

☰ Watch the video

4 GET THE PICTURE

A Check your answers to Exercise 3. Did you guess correctly?

B Check (✓) **True** or **False**. Correct the false statements.
Then compare with a partner.

	True	False	
1. Ellen heard a story at the restaurant.	☐	☐	....
2. Molly doesn't like scary stories.	☐	☐	....
3. The campground used to be a farm.	☐	☐	....
4. Ted McShane died in a fire.	☐	☐	....

5 WATCH FOR DETAILS

Complete the sentences. Then compare your answers with a partner.

1. Ellen overheard a woman telling this story to her .... _daughter_ ....

2. Vanessa tells Molly not to be a ....

3. The McShanes inherited the farm from a ....

4. When the McShanes walked down the street, they
   always.. .

5. Every evening, Mr. McShane brought his wife ....

6. Mr. McShane's wife was named ....

7. The girls get frightened when .... arrives.

6 MAKING INFERENCES

Which statements are probably true? Which are probably false? Check (✓) your
answers. Then compare with a partner.

	True	False
1. Vanessa likes scary stories.	☐	☐
2. The man in the story was a farmer.	☐	☐
3. The fire started because of a hot and dry summer.	☐	☐
4. The park ranger wanted to scare the girls.	☐	☐
5. Vanessa is embarrassed that they were so easily frightened.	☐	☐
6. The ranger is the same person from the story.	☐	☐

Follow-up

7 DO YOU BELIEVE THESE STORIES?

GROUP WORK Read the descriptions of the creatures below. Do you believe
they ever existed? Do you think they exist now? Have conversations like this:

A: Do you think the Loch Ness Monster exists?
B: I think it's just a story. There are no such things as monsters!
C: I hate to disagree, but many people say that they have seen strange creatures.

The Loch Ness Monster, Scotland

Alien Big Cats, England

This creature was first seen in 565 BCE, and
sightings are still reported every year. Some people
believe that it is a dinosaur, an eel, or a type of
whale. Many photos of "Nessie" have been taken,
but some have turned out to be fakes and others
are too dark or blurry to really show the creature.

Some people believe that large, wild cats, such as
panthers and leopards, exist in some areas of the
English countryside. Called "alien" because they are
foreign (not extraterrestrial!), none has ever been
captured. Photos and videos have never been clear
enough to prove their existence, yet there have
been as many as 2,000 sightings in a single year.

Interchange VRB 3 © Cambridge University Press 2012 Photocopiable

8 WHAT DID THEY SAY?

Watch the video and complete the conversation. Then practice it.

The ranger surprises the girls while Ellen is telling the story.

Ranger: Oh, I'm .... I didn't mean to ....
you ladies. I was making my .... and
.... to see if .... is all right.

Molly: Yes. A park ranger, of .... Yes, everything's ....
Ellen was .... us a .... story when you came by.

Ranger: Campfire .... , huh? That's .... fun. Well, OK, then.
I'll let you .... back to it.

Vanessa: Thanks for .... on us. And sorry .... the ....

Ranger: That's OK. I'm .... to it. Hey, in the .... you ....
should take a look .... that path. There's a .... full of
wildflowers, and .... in bloom right now – very ....

Vanessa: Oh! That's good to .... We'll .... that. Thanks.

9 PAST TENSE VERBS *Telling a story*

A Write the correct form of the verbs in parentheses
(past perfect, past continuous, or simple past) to
complete this story.

Last Saturday, I .... (walk) down Elm Street when I
.... (notice) something strange. A very fancy sports car
.... (sit) in front of the entrance to the First Bank building. No
one .... (be) in the car, but the engine ....
(run). I .... (stop) next to the car to take a look. It was the
first time I .... (see) a car like that. Suddenly, a man with a
large bag .... (run) out of the bank and
.... (jump) into the car. He .... (drive)
away so fast, he almost .... (hit) me. Then I realized:
I .... (witness) a bank robbery!

B PAIR WORK

A: Think of something unusual that has happened to you.
   Tell a story about what happened.
B: Listen and ask questions. Then change roles.

Travel World

1 CULTURE

Culture shock, the emotional and physical distress you may feel when you visit a foreign country or culture, has three stages. The first stage, sometimes called the "honeymoon" stage, is characterized by exaggerated happiness and excitement. In the second stage, you might feel angry or sad at not being able to communicate or understand the other culture. You might even get physically ill. Finally, in the third stage, you realize that the new culture offers rewards as well as challenges, and you feel ready and able to adapt to a new lifestyle.

Have you ever seen a visitor to your country experiencing culture shock? What kind of person do you think experiences culture shock the most severely? the least severely? Have you ever experienced culture shock? Describe your experiences.

2 VOCABULARY *Travel abroad*

Put the words below in the word map. Add at least one more word to each list. Then compare answers with a partner.

✓afraid to make a mistake	eating a huge meal at lunch	shaking hands
beautiful	kissing in public	spectacular
confused	picturesque	surprised

Customs

Travel Abroad

Feelings
afraid to make a mistake

Scenery

3 GUESS THE FACTS

What things do you think cause people to experience culture shock?

- ☐ climate
- ☐ clothing
- ☐ families
- ☐ food
- ☐ greetings
- ☐ hotels
- ☐ language
- ☐ transportation

☰ Watch the video

4 GET THE PICTURE

A Check your answers from Exercise 3. Then compare with a partner.

B Complete the information for each person.

Camilla

Lives in: ....
Visited: ....

Andrew

Is from: ....
Lives in: ....

Delfino

Is from: ....
Lives in: ....

5 GUESSING MEANING FROM CONTEXT

Read these sentences from the video. Guess the meanings of the underlined words.
Check (✓) your answers. Then compare with a partner.

1. When you get home, you often have some interesting and perhaps humorous stories to tell about your cross-cultural experiences.
   - ☐ experiences that made you angry
   - ✓ experiences in different cultures
   - ☐ experiences in similar cultures

2. Rio de Janeiro – that picturesque city of beautiful beaches, Carnaval, and the samba.
   - ☐ old-fashioned
   - ☐ expensive
   - ☐ pretty

3. You're invading my space.
   - ☐ making me uncomfortable
   - ☐ taking too much of my time
   - ☐ causing me pain

4. It is customary in my culture to have a huge meal in the middle of the day.
   - ☐ rare
   - ☐ polite
   - ☐ usual

6 WATCH FOR DETAILS

According to the video, to which country do the following customs refer?
Write the name of a country next to each custom.

Brazil   Sweden
Mexico   the United States
Peru

1. People shake hands when they meet.   ....

2. It's customary to eat a huge meal around noon.   ....

3. People kiss on the cheek when they meet.   ....

4. People often eat just a soup and sandwich for lunch. ....

5. Bus drivers call out to people on the street.   ....

7 WHAT'S YOUR OPINION?

A Which customs and situations discussed in the video would make you
feel uncomfortable when visiting a foreign country? Rank them from
1 (most uncomfortable) to 6 (least uncomfortable).

.... using public transportation   .... having only soup and a sandwich for lunch

.... greeting someone by kissing on the cheeks   .... using a private bus system

.... eating a huge meal in the middle of the day .... greeting someone by shaking hands

B **PAIR WORK** Take turns talking about the customs. Use sentences like these:

One thing I'd be most uncomfortable about . . .   The thing that I'd be most uncomfortable about . . .
Something I wouldn't be uncomfortable about . . .   The thing that I'd be least uncomfortable about . . .

Follow-up

8 CROSSING CULTURES

A Choose a country you know well. Make a list of customs that visitors to that
country might find different or unusual. Complete the chart.

Country	Customs	
....	....	....
	....	....

B **PAIR WORK** Take turns asking about the customs in the countries you and
your partner chose in part A.

Interchange VRB 3 © Cambridge University Press 2012   Photocopiable

9 *WHAT DID HE SAY?*

Watch the video to complete the commentary. Then compare with a partner.

Chris Brooks talks about culture shock.

Hi. I'm Chris Brooks. .... to *Travel World*. Have you ever

.... to a .... with a ....

different .... ? If you have, you .... know what

"................................" is. It's a feeling of .... you get

from .... being in a new .... The ....

and .... may seem .... are

different. You don't know exactly what you're .... do.

You may .... be a little .... of

 making a .... In .... , you get ....

.... everything. But .... you get .... ,

you often have some .... and perhaps .... stories

to .... about your .... experiences.

10 **EXPECTATIONS** *Noun, adjective, and verb forms*

A Complete the sentences about expectations with the correct word in parentheses.

1. It is .... (tradition / traditional) to have a large meal at noon in Mexico.

2. You are .... (expected / expectation) to kiss people on both cheeks in Brazil.

3. It is .... (custom / customary) for people to take public transportation in Peru.

4. Are you .... (suppose / supposed) to kiss people on both cheeks in Mexico?

5. My family has a .... (tradition / traditional) of eating dessert at every meal.

6. What is the .... (custom / customary) of greeting
   people in your country?

7. I didn't have any .... (expect / expectations) about
   what life was like in Peru.

8. What do you .... (suppose / supposed) I
   should do when I want more food?

B (PAIR WORK) Compare your statements with a partner.

6 What's the problem?

1 CULTURE

Travelers in North America looking for quaint, old-fashioned charm or personalized service sometimes choose to stay in a bed and breakfast, or "B & B." Herb and Ruth Boven opened Castle in the Country in Allegan, Michigan. "Our guests come here to relax, enjoy the countryside, or shop at antique markets and specialty shops," says Ruth. Castle in the Country offers special mystery or romance weekends and services such as horse-drawn wagon rides and holiday dinners. "We enjoy meeting guests from different states and countries and showing them what's special about our area."

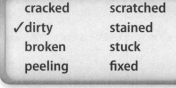

Have you ever stayed in a B & B? Would you like to stay in one? Talk about different types of hotels in your country with your classmates.

2 VOCABULARY *Problems*

Complete the sentences with words from the box. Then match each sentence with a picture. Compare with a partner.

cracked	scratched
✓dirty	stained
broken	stuck
peeling	fixed

1. The room needs cleaning. It's very ......dirty........ .
2. The paint is coming off the walls. It's ....
3. Oh, no. I spilled jam on my shirt. Now it's ....
4. My cat sharpened her claws on the table. Now it's ....
5. I dropped the glass on the floor and now it's ....
6. I can't open the window. It's ....
7. The remote control works now. It's ....
8. The cup isn't completely broken, but it is ....

Interchange VRB 3 © Cambridge University Press 2012   Photocopiable

3 GUESS THE STORY

Check (✓) what you think is happening in each of the following situations.

☐ The older man is checking in.
☐ The older man is giving instructions.

☐ The couple is here to relax.
☐ The couple is here on business.

☐ The man is calling home.
☐ The man is calling the front desk.

Watch the video

4 GET THE PICTURE

Complete the chart. Check (✓) the word that describes each problem.
More than one answer may be possible.

	broken	dirty	peeling	scratched	stuck
1. temperature control	☐	☐	☐	☐	☐
2. paint	☐	☐	☐	☐	☐
3. furniture	☐	☐	☐	☐	☐
4. window	☐	☐	☐	☐	☐
5. rug	☐	☐	☐	☐	☐

5 WATCH FOR DETAILS

Complete the sentences with **George**, **Norman**, **Ed**, or **Michelle**.

1. .... needs to go to the hardware store.

2. .... says they don't have much luggage.

3. .... thinks the front desk clerk is strange.

4. .... checks the couple into the hotel.

5. .... calls the front desk to report a problem.

6. .... tries to repair the window.

7. .... says it feels cold in the room.

8. .... returns after the guests leave.

6 WHAT'S YOUR OPINION?

PAIR WORK Answer these questions.

1. Do you agree with Michelle and Ed's decision to check out of the hotel?
   What would you have done?
2. Think of an experience you've had where there were problems. What were
   the problems? What did you do to solve them?

Follow-up

7 ROLE PLAY

A PAIR WORK How many problems can you find in the picture below? Take turns describing the problems to each other.

B GROUP WORK Now join another pair. Three of you are customers.
The fourth person is the waiter.

 Customers: Complain to the waiter about the problems in the restaurant.

 Waiter: Offer solutions to the customers' complaints.

Start like this:

Customer 1: Excuse me, but our dinners are cold.

 Waiter: Oh, I'm sorry. I'll take them back and heat them up.

Customer 2: OK. That would be fine.

Customer 3: Actually, could I order something else instead?

8 *WHAT DID THEY SAY?*

Watch the video and complete the conversation. Then practice it.

Ed and Michelle complain to Norman about their room.

Norman: Hi. What's the .... ?

Michelle: Oh, it's ....

Norman: .... the heat.

Ed: The heat ....

Norman: Well, what's .... with it?

Michelle: The dial's .... It came off in my ....

Norman: That should .... it.

Ed: .... That window needs .... , too.

It's .... and it's letting the .... air in.

Norman: That should .... it.

Michelle: .... ?

Norman: You're ....

9 NEED *WITH PASSIVE INFINITIVES AND GERUNDS*

A Read the list of additional problems at the hotel that Norman needs to fix. Then write two sentences with *need* for each problem. Use the verbs in the box.

Norman's List
- ☐ the heat is stuck on high
- ☐ the wastebasket is full
- ☐ the chair is damaged
- ☐ the hair dryer is broken
- ☐ the rooms are dirty
- ☐ the floors are dirty

✓adjust	fix
clean	repair
empty	wash

1. The heat needs adjusting. / The heat needs to be adjusted.

2. ....

3. ....

4. ....

5. ....

6. ....

B Now think of two things that need to be done at your school or at your home. Then write two sentences to describe what needs to be done.

1. ....

2. ....

Endangered islands

Preview

1 CULTURE

Scientists estimate that the average temperature on Earth has increased by about 0.6 degrees Celsius (one degree Fahrenheit) in the last century. They call this phenomenon global warming, or climate change. Sea levels have risen dramatically because of global warming, increasing as much as eight inches in some places. Low-lying areas and islands are in danger of being covered by the rising water. Some experts predict that if the rising tides continue, many islands and coastal areas around the world will become uninhabitable.

What do you know about the causes of global warming? What effect do you think rising sea levels might have on your country? What other effects do you think global warming might have?

2 VOCABULARY *Environmental change*

Complete the sentences with phrases from the box. Compare with a partner.

✓catastrophic event	coastal areas	global warming
climate panel	high tide	technological fix

1. Less than two days after the levees broke in New Orleans during Hurricane Katrina, 80 percent of the city was under water.
   It was a ....*catastrophic event*.... .

2. Engineers are likely to search for a .... to a problem, rather than a natural solution or a change in how people behave.

3. Tsunamis are usually more damaging to the .... of a country than the inland areas.

4. The government appointed a .... made up of scientific experts to find out how changing weather patterns might affect the country in the future.

5. Many scientists believe that .... is causing the glaciers to melt.

6. During a .... , many areas by the ocean that are usually above ground may be under water.

3 GUESS THE FACTS

Watch the first two minutes of the video with the sound off. Which of the following
do you think are concerns of people living on the island of Tuvalu?

- ☐ cold water
- ☐ flooding
- ☐ high tides
- ☐ hot weather
- ☐ unsafe drinking water
- ☐ strong winds

≡ Watch the video

4 GET THE PICTURE

A Look at your answers to Exercise 3. Did you guess correctly? Correct your
answers. Then compare with a partner.

B What are some threats faced by the people living on Tuvalu? Match
each threat with the correct picture.

1. Forecasts show that the tides will continue to
   get higher.
2. The main roads on the island are
   sometimes flooded.

3. The airport runway may disappear.
4. Plants won't grow in the salty water.

5 WATCH FOR DETAILS

Fill in the blanks. Then compare with a partner.

1. It's difficult to grow anything on Tuvalu because the soil is too ....

2. An Australian system has been monitoring the tides in Tuvalu for .... years.

3. Scientists predict that most coastal areas of Tuvalu will be washed out in .... years.

4. A typical high tide reaches about .... meters.

5. The highest point on Tuvalu is only about .... meters.

6. Without help, Tuvalu can survive for only about .... more years.

7. The island nation of Tuvalu has .... inhabitants.

6 GUESSING MEANING FROM CONTEXT

Read these sentences from the video. Choose the best meaning of each underlined word. Check (✓) your answers. Then compare with a partner.

1. Incredibly beautiful, but incredibly <u>vulnerable</u>.
   - ☐ expensive
   - ☐ easily damaged
   - ☐ ancient

2. The water also <u>surges up</u> from underground, through the coral the islands are built on.
   - ☐ floats
   - ☐ moves sideways
   - ☐ rises suddenly

3. This isn't like other floods that I've covered, with a single <u>catastrophic</u> event.
   - ☐ fortunate
   - ☐ terrible
   - ☐ interesting

4. At the harbor, the rising swell is <u>monitored</u> by an Australian system.
   - ☐ controlled
   - ☐ ignored
   - ☐ measured

5. These [islands] are so narrow, you can cross from one side to the other in a few short <u>paces</u>.
   - ☐ steps
   - ☐ miles
   - ☐ minutes

Follow-up

7 FOR OR AGAINST

A **PAIR WORK** Imagine you are in charge of an organization that is considering helping the island nation of Tuvalu. List three reasons for and against trying to save these islands.

For	Against
....	....
....	....
....	....

B **GROUP WORK** Now join another pair. Discuss the reasons you listed. Use language like this:

In my opinion . . .	On the other hand . . .
That's an interesting idea. However, . . .	That's a good point. Nevertheless, . . .
I feel that . . .	I don't think that . . .

Interchange VRB 3 © Cambridge University Press 2012   Photocopiable

8 WHAT DID HE SAY?

Watch the video and complete the commentary. Then compare with a partner.

A reporter is talking about what Tuvalu needs to survive.

For the children of Tuvalu, the .... are fun. But for them to .... their .... on these islands will require .... international .... And with .... 11,000 people here, will the .... world think it's .... it? Now, of course, Tuvalu does get some .... , but not .... enough to keep the .... sea at bay. So the .... community .... very soon a difficult .... of .... to draw a line between .... who get .... and those who don't. And in the .... , people here are getting ready for .... king tide. Right now it's .... ; it's due to get very .... in about eight hours' time.

9 THE PASSIVE

Rewrite these sentences from the active to the passive. Use the prepositions in parentheses to indicate the cause. Then compare with a partner.

1. King tides are washing out some of Tuvalu's coastal areas. (because of)

   Some of Tuvalu's coastal areas are being washed out because of king tides.

2. Salty seawater is killing off most of the plant life. (due to)

   ....

   ....

3. An Australian system monitors the changes in sea level on Tuvalu. (by)

   ....

   ....

4. In five to ten years, rising sea levels will cover many coastal areas. (as a result of)

   ....

   ....

5. The international community must set up a global fund to save Tuvalu. (by)

   ....

   ....

8 Tango!

Preview

1 CULTURE

Tango dancing began in Argentina and Uruguay in the mid-1800s. The music of tango blended African, Cuban, and European elements. Over time, tango music and tango dancing united people from many different cultures and social classes in South America. As sailors from Argentina traveled to Europe and North America, they taught the dance to local residents, and its popularity spread. Today there are tango schools all over the world, and new styles of the dance are constantly evolving. One of the latest styles, *nuevo tango*, brings in electronic and alternative music and adds new life to this ever-popular dance form.

Why do you think people like to dance? Give as many reasons as you can. What kinds of dances are popular in your country? What kinds have you tried? What kinds of music are popular in your country now? Are there dances that go with each type of music?

2 VOCABULARY Learning

A **PAIR WORK** What are some phrases used to talk about learning? Match each verb on the left to a word or phrase on the right.

1. decide to   to ski
2. earn   take lessons
3. brush up on   hitting the ball
4. learn how   a diploma
5. practice   classes
6. take   my skills

B Complete the sentence below with phrases from part A. Change the verb form if necessary.

1. I heard you're interested in playing the violin. Did you

   decide to take lessons ?

2. If you want to get better at tennis, you'll have to .... !

3. I already know how to do karate, but I'm taking lessons just to ....

4. It's hard to learn to dance by myself. I'm going to .... with a friend.

5. Kim graduated from college last May. She .... in engineering.

6. This winter, James wants to ....

3 GUESS THE FACTS

Why do you think tango dancing is so popular? What are some ways people can learn or improve tango dancing?

Watch the video

4 GET THE PICTURE

What reasons do people give for wanting to learn the tango? Check (✓) your answers. Then compare with a partner.

☐ They're just interested in dancing.
☐ Their friends told them to learn the tango.
☐ They want to keep fit and have fun.

☐ The tango is exotic and challenging.
☐ They didn't like any other dances.
☐ The tango has a great rhythm.

5 WATCH FOR DETAILS

How do these people recommend learning or improving tango dancing? Match each person with a recommendation.

.... By starting with group classes or private classes.
.... By practicing with a guy.
.... By going to a tango club.

.... By practicing hard.
.... By taking the initiative and taking a class.

6 WHAT'S YOUR OPINION?

A How important do you think these qualities are for learning to dance?
Rank them from 1 (most important) to 9 (least important).

.... athletic ability   .... curiosity   .... patience

.... competitiveness   .... intelligence   .... self-confidence

.... creativity   .... motivation   .... willpower

B **PAIR WORK** Compare your answers with a partner. Explain how you made
your choices. Then talk about these activities. Would your rankings change?
Why or why not?

learning a foreign language   learning to play tennis   learning to cook

☰ Follow-up

7 ADVICE TO LEARNERS

A Think of a sport, game, or activity that you have learned.
Make a list of different ways to learn it.

Activity ....

Ways to learn

B **GROUP WORK** Take turns asking and answering questions about the activities
the group members have chosen. Use language like this:

How did you learn to . . . ?   I learned . . . by . . .
Why do you enjoy . . . ?   I enjoy . . . because . . .
What's the best way to learn . . . ?   The best way to learn . . . is by . . .
What's a good way to improve . . . ?   A good way to improve . . . is to . . .

8 *WHAT DID THEY SAY?*

Watch the video and complete the conversation. Then practice with a partner.

A dance teacher talks about learning the tango.

Kevin: Why do you think tango is so .... ?

Uche: I think tango is .... because it's very .... and it's also very .... for people, and once people .... something that they find .... and it's very .... , I think they .... very rewarded.

Kevin: What do you .... for people who .... to learn tango?

Uche: I would recommend starting with .... classes or .... classes.

Kevin: And .... you've learned the .... of tango, what's a good way to .... your moves?

Uche: By going out .... with the people that you've .... the .... with, ... at home, listening to the .... , just feeling very .... with the music, and then .... dancing again.

9 *GERUNDS AND INFINITIVES* Talking about preferences

A For each pair of expressions, complete the questions.

1. earn a degree / learn for fun
   Would you prefer *to earn a degree or learn for fun* .... ?
2. learn English in Australia / in Canada
   Would you rather .... ?
3. learn how to cook / how to dance the tango
   Would you prefer .... ?
4. brush up on skills you already have / learn something new
   Would you rather .... ?
5. read English magazines / English novels
   Would you rather .... ?
6. study in the morning / at night
   Would you prefer .... ?

B **GROUP WORK** Ask several classmates the questions in part A. Then share their answers with the class.

"Mari would prefer to start a business. Juan would rather learn to dance at home."

9 Stressed out

Preview

1 CULTURE

What is stress? There are three main types:
- Mechanical stress, caused by carrying heavy objects, not getting enough exercise, or sleep disorders.
- Mental stress, caused by things such as relationship problems, financial worries, or career concerns.
- Chemical stress, caused by air and water pollution, detergents and cleaning products, and chemicals used in manufacturing.

Our bodies react to stress with the "fight or flight" response; you may want to challenge what stresses you, or you may want to run away!

What other kinds of mechanical, mental, and chemical stresses can you think of? Make a list with a partner or group. How many of these do you think affect you? What are some solutions to stress? What is your favorite way to relax?

2 VOCABULARY Stress

Choose from the expressions in the box to complete the paragraph below. Each expression is used only once.

blow off steam	in knots	take some time off	very relaxing
get some exercise	✓ stressed out	under pressure	what I needed

Last year, I felt completely ....stressed out................ by my job. Every day it

seemed like I was .... from my boss. My stomach was

.... all the time. I used to ....

by complaining to my co-workers, but that only made them feel stressed,

too! Someone in my office said I should .... ,

but I felt too tired to go. Finally, my boss suggested, "Why don't you

.... and go to a health spa for a few days? It'll be

...." It turned out to be just .... !

When I got back, I felt calm and ready to handle anything.

Interchange VRB 3 © Cambridge University Press 2012   Photocopiable

Watch the first minute of the video with the sound off.
Answer these questions.

1. What is the woman's problem?
2. What do you think the man is telling her?

Watch the video

4 **GET THE PICTURE**

A Check (✓) the suggestions for stress relief that Carmen and Hugo talk about.

aromatherapy

dance lessons

hypnotherapy

ice-skating

sleeping

swimming

taking a vacation

talking to friends

yoga

B **PAIR WORK** Which of the activities above have you tried? Which would you like to try?

5 **WATCH FOR DETAILS**

Why doesn't Carmen like these suggestions for stress relief? Check (✓)
the reason Carmen rejects each suggestion.

1. skating ⬜ Her skate broke. ⬜ The lessons were expensive.
2. dance lessons ⬜ She couldn't find a partner. ⬜ She got hurt.
3. yoga ⬜ It was too slow. ⬜ It twisted her in knots.
4. hypnotherapy ⬜ It didn't work. ⬜ It worked too well.
5. aromatherapy ⬜ She's allergic to perfumes. ⬜ She already tried it.

6 WHAT'S YOUR OPINION?

A PAIR WORK Imagine that Hugo suggests these activities for reducing stress to Carmen. Write the reasons Carmen might give for rejecting them.

playing tennis	running	listening to music	doing aerobics
get hit by a ball			

B PAIR WORK Now act out Hugo and Carmen's conversation. Start like this:

Hugo: Have you thought about playing tennis?
Carmen: I've already tried that, but I got hit by the ball!

☰ Follow-up

7 HOW STRESSED ARE YOU?

A PAIR WORK How much stress do you feel in the situations below? Add one more idea and check (✓) your answers. Then compare with a partner. Have conversations like this:

A: How much stress do you feel at school?
B: A lot. I have too much homework every night. How about you?

	none at all	a little	some	a lot
1. at school	☐	☐	☐	☐
2. with friends	☐	☐	☐	☐
3. on weekends	☐	☐	☐	☐
4. when visiting relatives	☐	☐	☐	☐
5. when traveling	☐	☐	☐	☐
6. .... (your idea)	☐	☐	☐	☐

B CLASS ACTIVITY Ask your classmates about how much stress they feel in the situations. Check (✓) their answers in the chart. Which things are the most stressful? the least stressful?

8 WHAT DID THEY SAY?

Watch the video and complete the conversation. Then practice it.

Carmen and Hugo talk about some possible solutions to her problem.

Hugo: There's always ....

Carmen: I've tried that, too. Now, ... time I .... the word "ocean," it's supposed to .... me. Oh, and it .... ! The other day, I was in a .... Someone .... talking about the .... problems in the world's .... People said the .... "ocean" so many times, I ....

Hugo: Oh, yeah. I .... about that. That must've been ....

Carmen: Now half the .... knows. See what I mean? I .... to get the hypnotherapy ....

Hugo: I have an idea. You could .... aromatherapy.

Carmen: .... ?

Hugo: It's .... a massage, but they .... your skin .... scented oils.

9 SUGGESTIONS

A Hugo would like some advice for his problems. Write a suggestion for each of his problems. Use the expressions in the box.

Have you thought about . . . ?	**Maybe you could . . .**	**Why don't you . . . ?**
It might be a good idea to . . .	**One thing you could do is . . .**	**What about . . . ?**

1. I'd really like to learn Spanish, but I never seem to have enough time.

   ....

2. Sometimes I can't finish my work because I get too many phone calls.

   ....

3. I want to go on vacation next month, but the boss wants me to be in the office.

   ....

4. I'd like to do something interesting on my lunch hour.

   ....

5. I love to read at night, but I usually fall asleep as soon as I begin to read.

   ....

B **PAIR WORK** Write two problems you have for which you would like advice. Then take turns reading your problems and offering suggestions.

1. ....

2. ....

The Virtual Office

1 CULTURE

In today's world, people have more choices than ever about where they do their jobs. Many companies are still located in office buildings, but the convenience of the Internet gives businesses new and exciting options. Many jobs, like website development and public relations, can be done from home, a café, or anywhere there's an Internet connection. Some companies also encourage employees to use instant messaging, online discussions, and video conferencing to communicate effectively with co-workers and clients.

What are some virtual jobs you know about? Do you think all jobs will become virtual someday? Why do you think people might not want to work in an office building?

2 VOCABULARY *Today's office*

Match the word in the box to the correct picture below.

commute	kiosk
corporate headquarters	meeting
cyberspace	✓ workspace

1
.... workspace ....

2
....

3
....

4
....

5
....

6
....

3 GUESS THE FACTS

What percentage of employees at IBM do you think work somewhere outside the office?

Watch the video

4 GET THE PICTURE

A Check your answer to Exercise 3. How close was your guess?

B Check (✓) **True** or **False**. Correct the false statements. Then compare with a partner.

	True	False	
1. IBM has 250,000 employees.	☐	☐	....
2. Bob Flavin works as a volunteer at an ambulance corps.	☐	☐	....
3. The CEO of Accenture has an office with his name on the door.	☐	☐	....
4. Accenture employees can reserve a workspace if they need it.	☐	☐	....
5. Crayon's workers often meet in the physical world.	☐	☐	....
6. The reporter met Crayon's CEO in person.	☐	☐	....

5 MAKING INFERENCES

Which statements are probably true? Which are probably false?
Check (✓) your answers and compare with a partner.

	True	False
1. Bob Flavin works in the same office every day.	☐	☐
2. Bob Flavin likes working outside the regular office.	☐	☐
3. Janet Hoffman would like to have a big comfortable office.	☐	☐
4. Crayon Marketing has an office building with a rooftop space for parties.	☐	☐
5. Crayon workers communicate with each other regularly.	☐	☐
6. Joseph Jaffe believes that regular offices are necessary.	☐	☐

Which new ideas about working were mentioned in the video? Check (✓) all the correct answers. Then write one more idea of your own.

1. Meetings in cyberspace ☐
2. Playing video games in the workplace ☐
3. Reserving a workspace only when you need it ☐
4. Bringing people together, no matter where they are in the world ☐
5. Cloud computing ☐
6. Having a virtual office party ☐
7. ....

Follow-up

7 CREATE YOUR OWN VIRTUAL OFFICE

A Imagine you have a new job where you work outside the traditional office building. Complete the chart with the location of the job, when it would begin and end, how you would stay in touch with colleagues, and how you would hold meetings.

Your job: ....

Location	Hours	Colleagues	Meetings
....	....	....	....
....	....	....	....
....	....	....	....

B PAIR WORK Compare your answers in part A with your partner.

A: What is your new job?
B: I am a web developer. I work from home. . . .

8 WHAT DID THEY SAY?

Watch the video and complete the commentary. Then compare with a partner.

A TV anchor introduces reporter Betsey Stark and her story on the virtual office.

Anchor: Finally from us, the virtual office. For better or .... ,
technology and .... are creating startling
.... in what it .... to be " ....
...." Betsey Stark is tracking the
.... order of .... and ....
begins our series, "The .... of Work."

Reporter: Imagine a work .... with no commute, no
corporate ...., maybe no .... in the
.... world at all. For Bob Flavin, Janet Hoffman,
and Joseph Jaffe, the .... is .... here.

Bob Flavin: These days we .... so .... stuff by
.... and things, um, that it ....
where you ....

9 PAST, PRESENT, AND FUTURE

A Complete the sentences below. Use the correct preposition or the correct form
of the verb in parentheses.

1. ....**In**........ the 1960s, people listened to music on record players. Nowadays, people mostly
.............**use**............ (use) MP3 players. Some experts believe that people in the future
.... (listen) to music through chips in their brains.

2. .... the Middle Ages, most people have lived in rural areas and towns. However, this trend
.... (change). In fact, most people now .... (live) in cities.

3. .... many years, people didn't spend time on computers and mobile devices. Now, of
course, they .... (be) common. Some experts think that in the next few years,
most people .... (spend) almost 60 hours a week on electronic devices!

B (PAIR WORK) Write two sentences based on the
information in the table. Then compare your answers
with a partner.

Average human lifespan		
1900	**Now**	**2050**
50 years	78 years	84 years

1. In 2050, people will live longer than they do now. ....

2. ....

3. ....

11 Live and learn

1 CULTURE

Most people remember at least one time when they made an embarrassing mistake – oversleeping and missing an exam, spilling food at a dinner party, calling someone by the wrong name. These mistakes can feel awful at the time. However, experts say that worrying too much about mistakes can keep people from trying new things. Some science suggests that the brain needs to do things incorrectly in order to build new knowledge. In the words of John Enoch Powell,, "The only real mistake is the one from which we learn nothing."

How do you feel when you make a mistake? Do you forget about it quickly, or think about it a lot afterward? What advice would you give a friend who made a mistake?

2 VOCABULARY *Mistakes at work*

A Put the words in the chart. Then add one more word to each list.

advertising agency	meeting	technology company
✓conference	performance	theater
embarrassed	spellbound	unprofessional

Events	Types of businesses	Feelings
conference		

B **PAIR WORK** Think about a mistake you made in the past in school or at work. Then take turns asking and answering the questions below.

1. What was the mistake you made?
2. How did the mistake make you feel?
3. What did you learn from the mistake?

3 GUESS THE STORY

Watch the first minute of the video with the sound off. What question do you think the interviewer is asking?

Watch the video

4 GET THE PICTURE

Where did these people's stories take place? Write it under the picture.
Add two more pieces of information about each person's story.

Amber

Evan

Alexis

Where: .... Where: .... Where: ....
Other: .... Other: .... Other: ....
....

5 WATCH FOR DETAILS

Check (✓) **True** or **False**. Then correct the false statements. Compare with a partner.

	True	False	
1. Amber was still in college.	☐	☐	....
2. Amber was embarrassed at lunch.	☐	☐	....
3. Amber was wearing sandals.	☐	☐	....
4. Evan was on vacation.	☐	☐	....
5. Evan was staying with an old friend.	☐	☐	....
6. Evan broke a lamp.	☐	☐	....
7. Alexis took tickets at the theater.	☐	☐	....
8. Alexis's phone rang very quietly.	☐	☐	....

6 MAKING INFERENCES

Which statements are probably true? Which are probably false? Check (✓) your answers.
Then compare with a partner. Give reasons for your answers.

	True	False
1. Amber knew what the office dress codes were.	☐	☐
2. Amber worries a lot about her past mistakes.	☐	☐
3. Evan didn't mean to break the vase.	☐	☐
4. Evan bought a new vase to replace the one he broke.	☐	☐
5. Alexis likes hip-hop music.	☐	☐
6. Alexis usually turns off her cell phone during a performance.	☐	☐

Follow-up

7 I SHOULD HAVE . . .

A Make notes about two situations in which you or someone you know made
a mistake or did something embarrassing. Then suggest one or two things the
person could or should have done differently.

Situation	I should have . . .
I was late to my sister's wedding.	I should have set my alarm clock.
	I should have asked my brother to wake me up.

B **PAIR WORK** Take turns sharing your situations and solutions.
Talk about what happened and what the person should have done.

8 *WHAT DID HE SAY?*

Watch the video and complete the story. Then compare with a partner.

Evan talks about an embarrassing moment in his life.

I was attending a .... out of town and .... with
an old friend, Ed, and his .... The first morning,
I .... I was rushing to leave the ....
when I knocked over a .... and .... it.
No one was awake yet, and I was ....
.... , so I just threw away the .... By the time I
.... it up, I was really .... , so I left.
I .... Ed and told him
about it, but, honestly, I .... That night, when I got back to
the .... , Ed and his wife, Michelle, were having an ....
with their son, Ben. They thought Ben .... the
vase and then tried to .... it.

9 *PAST CONDITIONALS*

A Rewrite the sentences using **if** clauses + past perfect.

1. I didn't go to bed early, so I fell asleep during the test.
   If I had gone to bed early, I wouldn't have fallen asleep during the test.

2. She took summer classes, so she graduated early.

   ....

3. He didn't know the answer, so he was embarrassed.

   ....

4. They brought a map, so they didn't get lost.

   ....

5. You didn't hear the announcement, so you missed your train.

   ....

6. We bought a new car, so we didn't have money for a vacation.

   ....

B **GROUP WORK** Talk about how your life would have
been different if . . .

your parents had been millionaires.
you had been born a member of the opposite sex.
you had lived 200 years ago.
you had never gone to school.

12 Good business

1 CULTURE

Cafés are very popular in North America. In a café or coffeehouse, customers can sit for hours in a comfortable chair, talk with friends, and drink coffee. Many cafés are small, family-run businesses, but others are part of a chain run by a larger company. Some studies show that when a coffeehouse chain opens a store, the smaller coffee shops in the neighborhood attract more business as well. It may be that seeing a new coffeehouse just reminds people how much they like visiting their favorite café.

What do you like about your favorite coffee shop or café? Is it close to your home, work, or school? Do they play nice music? What's your favorite thing to eat or drink there?

2 VOCABULARY A café

A **PAIR WORK** Complete the conversation with words from the box.

A: I'm looking for a place to get a ....*great*.......... cup of coffee.

B: How about Gino's Grind? It's nearby, so it's very ....

A: Do they have .... chairs?

B: Yes, they do. Gino's is small and .... It's .... with all the students.

A: I want to be able to have a conversation without shouting. Is the music very .... ?

B: No, it's not. And they have nice things to eat there, too. The owner makes .... pastries every morning.

A: That's good, but you know the real secret to a .... coffee shop is delicious coffee.

B: You said it! And Gino's coffee is fantastic. Let's go!

comfortable
convenient
cozy
fresh
✓great
loud
popular
successful

B **PAIR WORK** Take turns guessing the words in part A.

A: This word describes a place that is easy to get to.
B: Convenient.

3 GUESS THE FACTS

Who are these people?

1

- ☐ café owner
- ☐ reporter

2

- ☐ café owner
- ☐ reporter

☰ Watch the video

4 GET THE PICTURE

A Check the reasons the café owner gives for the success of her business.

- ☐ Students like to do their homework at the café.
- ☐ The café stays open late.
- ☐ The music is always good.

- ☐ There are comfortable chairs.
- ☐ They serve unusual foods.
- ☐ The café is close to campus.

B Match each picture to the correct description.

1. People can sit outside.
2. People come here to study or read.
3. The food is made fresh every morning.
4. The chairs are comfortable.

5 WATCH FOR DETAILS

Complete the sentences. Then compare your answers with a partner.

1. Lili is the .... of Choice Café.
2. Choice Cafe's .... makes it easy for students to find.
3. Central Café closed because ....
4. People come to drink a few cups of coffee and have ....
5. While some customers eat their food inside the café, others eat ....
6. Lili encourages people who come to the café to ....
7. The .... isn't too loud, so people can chat together or read.
8. Lili lets the .... who work at the café choose the music.

6 WHAT'S YOUR OPINION?

A **GROUP WORK** Ask three of your classmates what they think about cafés and coffee shops. Be sure to ask for reasons. Take notes in the chart.

	.... (name)	.... (name)	.... (name)
1 Do you think a café is a good place to study?			
2 Do you think most cafés are affordable?			
3 Do you enjoy meeting your friends at a café?			
4 Do you want to work at a café?			
5 (your own question)			

B Share your information with the class. Did any comments surprise you?

Follow-up

7 OPEN YOUR OWN CAFÉ

A **PAIR WORK** Make plans for opening your own café. Answer the questions.

What is the name of your business?
Where will it be located in your community?
How large will it be?
What hours will it be open?
What will the furniture be like?
What kind of music will be played?
What kind of foods will you serve?

B **GROUP WORK** Join another pair and take turns describing your cafés.

     Interchange VRB 3 © Cambridge University Press 2012   Photocopiable

8 *WHAT DID THEY SAY?*

Watch the video and complete the conversation. Then compare with a partner.

Jacob and Lili talk about the food and atmosphere at Choice Café.

Jacob: What .... the food?

Lili: Our food is made here .... every morning.
We have a .... take-out business. People
order food to take home or to eat ....

Jacob: .... ? You mean, on the .... ,
on campus?

Lili: .... We do have tables outside, too.
But .... do eat on campus. It's really
.... there.

Jacob: But it's nice to sit .... , too. The atmosphere is great ....
Talk about that for a minute: the .... , the ....

Lili: Music is key to a café's .... You need to ....
you have good music. I'm not an .... I mean, I don't
know .... about music. But people who work here are ....
They're .... They know what's .... So I let them
.... the music.

9 *INFINITIVE CLAUSES AND PHRASES OF PURPOSE*

A Complete these sentences about starting a café. Use **in order for** or **in order to**.

1. ....*In order to*......... open a café, you will probably need to borrow money.

2. .... the café to be legal, you need to get a license.

3. .... people to learn about the place, you will need to advertise.

4. .... make money, you have to charge enough money to cover your costs.

B Complete these sentences with **because, because of, for,** and **the reason**.

1. We decided to open a café ....*because*.......... we love coffee so much.

2. .... it took us so long to open our café was that we had to raise the money.

3. We had to open a week late .... a big storm in the area.

4. Now our café is known .... its fresh coffee and comfortable atmosphere.

Stonehenge

1 CULTURE

For reasons scientists do not completely understand, ancient cultures all around the world made monuments by arranging stones in a particular pattern. Archaeologists have discovered stone structures in Great Britain, Europe, South America, and Africa. Some, like the stone circles at Gobekli Tepe in Turkey, are also carved with designs and figures of animals and humans. Others, like Stonehenge in the United Kingdom, are exceptional because of their size and sophisticated engineering. Most of these monuments were created before written language. Archaeologists must use a wide variety of clues to uncover the true purpose for these amazing structures. In some cases, we may never know.

Have you ever visited an ancient historical site? What did it look like? Who built it?
Why was it built? What did you find particularly interesting or meaningful about your visit?

2 VOCABULARY *Ancient history*

Check (✓) the best meaning for the underlined word in each sentence.
Compare with a partner.

1. Anthropologists don't know how people could have built such <u>colossal</u> structures without the help of modern construction equipment.
   ☐ expensive ☐ beautiful ☑ huge

2. Experts found religious items at the ruins, which made them suspect it was a <u>shrine</u>.
   ☐ market ☐ holy place ☐ school

3. The creators of Stonehenge only had <u>primitive</u> tools, but their knowledge of engineering was sophisticated.
   ☐ useful ☐ basic ☐ metal

4. The Aztecs wore <u>ceremonial</u> masks with faces of their deities on them.
   ☐ used for business ☐ used for special rituals ☐ used in everyday life

5. After death, the <u>cremated remains</u> of important people were buried in a special graveyard.
   ☐ family members ☐ burned bodies ☐ clothes or possessions

6. The first scientists to <u>excavate</u> the ancient burial mound discovered very old pottery, tools, and weapons.
   ☐ cut down with a saw ☐ examine with binoculars ☐ uncover by digging out earth

3 GUESS THE FACTS

Watch the first minute of the video with the sound off. What kinds
of experts do you think will give opinions about Stonehenge?

☐ archaeologists   ☐ construction experts   ☐ historians
☐ astronomers   ☐ geologists   ☐ reporters

≡ **Watch the video**

4 GET THE PICTURE

A Match each fact to the correct picture.

a. Stonehenge is made up of colossal standing stones.
b. Archaeologists have uncovered hundreds of human bones.
c. A second circle called Blue Stonehenge was discovered.
d. Stonehenge may have been a temple of the dead.

....

B Write each phrase under the correct picture.

an excavation   a place to commune with the spirits
a monumental undertaking   a part of the ceremonial complex

5 WATCH FOR DETAILS

Check (✓) **True** or **False**. Then correct the false statements.
Compare with a partner.

	True	False	
1. Stonehenge is located in Wales.	☐	☐	....
2. Stonehenge contains about 53 standing stones.	☐	☐	....
3. Some of the stones weigh 40 tons.	☐	☐	....
4. Experts know who built Stonehenge.	☐	☐	....
5. Some people think Stonehenge was an alien landing site.	☐	☐	....
6. Most of the people buried at Stonehenge were men.	☐	☐	....
7. Blue Stonehenge was discovered in 2008.	☐	☐	....
8. Blue Stonehenge is shaped like a circle.	☐	☐	....

6 WHAT'S YOUR OPINION?

A Which of the sentences below do you think is the most likely explanation for the origin of Stonehenge? Rank them from 1 (most likely) to 5 (least likely).

.... It was built by aliens from another part of the universe.

.... It was a temple built to worship the sun.

.... It was a kind of hospital where sick people came to be healed.

.... It was a shrine, a holy place for the ancient Druid people who lived in the area.

.... It was a burial place where people came to commune with the dead.

B **PAIR WORK** Tell your partner which explanation you thought was the most likely, and why. Then talk about any other possible explanations for the building of Stonehenge.

Follow-up

7 WHAT DO YOU THINK HAPPENED?

A Read the descriptions of the mysterious events below.

What was the Tunguska event?

What happened to the Maya?

On June 30, 1908, a massive explosion took place in Siberia, Russia. Eighty million trees over an area of more than 2,000 square kilometers were destroyed by the blast. Some people believe that the destruction was caused by the crash of an alien spaceship. Scientists agree that it was caused by something from outer space, but they think it was a meteorite or a small comet.

Between the 8th and 9th centuries CE, the Mayan people in the lowlands of Central America suddenly abandoned many of their cities. Their disappearance is still a mystery. Some people believe that the Mayans fled after predicting the end of their own civilization. Archaeologists think that drought, foreign invasion, or disease might have caused the Mayan civilization in this area to collapse.

B **GROUP WORK** What do you think might have caused these mysterious events? Share your opinions with the group. Have conversations like this:

A: What do you think caused the Tunguska event?
B: I think it must have been a small comet.
C: I'm not sure. I think it could have been aliens.

   Interchange VRB 3 © Cambridge University Press 2012   Photocopiable

8 WHAT DID THEY SAY?

Watch the video to complete the commentary. Then compare with a partner.

Scientist Julian Richards talks about Stonehenge.

Julian Richards: The .... we're .... with here is our .... , and
what .... prehistory is that we've got no ....
.... about .... So ....
that we understand about it comes from archaeology,
from .... we can excavate and what we
can ....

Narrator: In 2008, ... of .... bones were
.... at the .... , primitively burned
and .... The bones were dated across a
.... years of prehistory.

Julian Richards: The first .... of all the cremated ....
that were .... at Stonehenge .... that it's ....
adult .... , adult men that were .... there. So it's quite a
.... group of people, and only probably very .... people
came .... to be buried.

9 PASSIVE AND PAST MODALS

Rewrite the sentences using the passive voice.

1. Ancient peoples must have used stone circles for rituals.
   Stone circles must have been used by ancient peoples for rituals.

2. Better farming practices might have saved the Mayan people.
   ....

3. An infectious disease could have killed the Mayans.
   ....

4. A small comet may have destroyed eighty million trees in Tunguska.
   ....

5. The builders of Stonehenge couldn't have used vehicles with wheels.
   ....

6. The discovery of a second circle at Stonehenge must have surprised archaeologists.
   ....

14 Making music

1 CULTURE

Musicians are always looking for new ways to share their music with the world. These days, they may not need a record contract to attract an audience. Many small bands and solo artists use the Internet as their musical outlet. They can upload their songs to a music-sharing website, so anyone with access to the Internet can hear their music. These innovations are allowing independent artists to get noticed online, and to connect with other musicians and new fans.

Where do you get the music you listen to – radio, the Internet, CDs, or other places? Do you ever go to concerts? Where do you hear about new music?

2 VOCABULARY *Writing and recording songs*

A Choose words from the box to complete the sentences.

accompany	mix	set up
✓ compose	record	tune

1. The first thing a songwriter must do is ......*compose*...... a song.

2. Before playing an electric piano, a musician must .... the keyboard.

3. Before playing a guitar, a musician must .... the instrument.

4. A piano player may .... a singer.

5. When musicians .... their songs, they can hear what they sound like.

6. At a recording studio, an engineer will .... the voices and instruments together.

B **PAIR WORK** Compare your answers. Take turns using the words from the box in original sentences.

Interchange VRB 3 © Cambridge University Press 2012   Photocopiable

3 GUESS THE FACTS

What do you think these people who work in the music industry do?

recording engineer   DJ   program director   accompanist

Watch the video

4 GET THE PICTURE

What is each person's job? Write it under the picture. Use the words in the box.

Josh McBride

....

Richard Marr

....

accompanist
DJ
program director
recording engineer
songwriter

Aldous Collins

....

Melanie Oliver

....

Matthew Hawkes

....

5 WATCH FOR DETAILS

A Complete the sentences with a job from Exercise 4.

1. The .... uses a multitrack recorder.

2. The .... speaks with listeners on the radio.

3. The .... plays along with the singer in the recording studio.

4. The .... writes music as a way to make sense of the world.

5. The .... decides what music is played on the air.

B **PAIR WORK** Tell your partner another detail about each of these jobs.

"The songwriter uses a thesaurus to write his songs."

6 WRITING A SONG

A Imagine that you are a songwriter, and you have just written a great new song. Write your answers to the questions below.

1. What is the song about?
2. What instrument(s) do you use on your song?
3. Where do you want to record the song?
4. How will people hear your song (on the radio, in clubs, on the Internet, other)?
5. Who do you want to listen to your song?

My new song

1.

2.

3.

4.

5.

B (PAIR WORK) Compare your song ideas with a partner. Explain the reasons for your decisions.

7 WHICH JOB WOULD YOU LIKE?

A (PAIR WORK) Which music industry job appeals to you most – a singer, a songwriter, a DJ, or something else? Tell your partner why you would be good at the job you chose.

B (GROUP WORK) Join another pair. Compare your choices. Give reasons for your decisions.

8 WHAT DID THEY SAY?

Watch the video and complete the commentaries. Then compare with a partner.

Two people in the music industry talk about their jobs.

Matthew: Making music is my .... outlet: the way I make

.... of the world .... me. ....

I sit down to .... , the first thing I do is .... my

guitar. Once the .... is tuned up and .... ,

I set up the keyboard. The .... has multiple

.... and multiple .... What comes

.... of .... is a .... of .... I'm

.... that .... Sometimes I can .... hours writing

.... piece. I'm .... this song. I .... it "Revelations."

*   *   *

Melanie: Hi, my name's Melanie Oliver. I'm the ....

here at the .... The program director's

job is to .... what music is .... on air.

So I .... the songs and tell the DJs ....

songs to play.

9 PASSIVE *How a song becomes a hit*

A Complete the sentences below about how a song becomes a hit by using the passive form of the verbs in parentheses.

.... The song .... (record) on a multitrack recorder.

.... The song .... (play) on the radio by the DJ.

.... The recording .... (take) to program directors at radio stations

and .... (add) to their playlists.

...1... The song .... (compose) by the songwriter.

.... The song .... (choose) for airplay by the program director.

.... The vocals and instruments .... (mix) together.

B **PAIR WORK** Put the sentences above in order. Then take turns describing how a song becomes a hit. Use **first**, **next**, **then**, **after that**, and **finally**.

15 The streets of Montreal

1 CULTURE

Most North Americans rely on their cars for transportation, but recently more people are choosing to ride their bicycles to work instead. Some cities are investing in bicycle paths and other changes to the roads, so it's easy and safe for cyclists to get around. Why are more people cycling to work? Cyclists say it improves physical fitness, protects the environment, and cuts down on traffic noise and crowding. Plus, there's an added benefit: It's fun!

How do you feel about cycling? Do you ever cycle to work or to school? How would you like drivers of cars to change their behavior? What would you like to see cyclists do differently?

2 VOCABULARY City traffic

Complete these sentences with the words in the box. Use the plural form when necessary.

bike helmet	bus	cycle path	cyclist	commuter
driver	traffic	parking	pedestrian	✓sidewalk

1. People walking on the ....sidewalk............ avoid traffic from bicycles and cars.

2. Some .... take the train to work every day.

3. .... should always keep their bicycles in good repair.

4. .... generally stay on the sidewalk.

5. Cyclists should not ride into oncoming ....

6. As more bicycles crowd the roads, ... have to share the road with cyclists.

7. .... reduce traffic and encourage public transportation.

8. Every cyclist should wear a ....

9. A .... is the safest place for cyclists to ride.

10. Drivers who commute to work may have trouble finding a .... spot.

Interchange VRB 3 © Cambridge University Press 2012 Photocopiable

3 GUESS THE FACTS

Watch the first minute of the video with the sound off.
Answer these questions.

1. Who is this man?
2. Where is he?
3. What do you think he's talking to people about?

Watch the video

4 GET THE PICTURE

Which issue does each person discuss? Check (✓) your answers.

☐ Cycle paths
☐ Listening to music

☐ Bicycles and buses
☐ Driving toward traffic

☐ Cycling with children
☐ Restricting driving downtown

☐ Checking mirrors
☐ Cycling with children

☐ Bicycles and buses
☐ Driving toward traffic

☐ Wearing bike helmets
☐ Riding with headphones

☐ Cycle paths
☐ Cycling with children

5 WHO SAID WHAT?

Who said the sentences below? Match each person from Exercise 4 with a sentence.
Then compare with a partner.

.... "I think it would be best if bicycles and buses were not on the same street."
.... "Cyclists should have their own bike lane and drive towards the oncoming traffic."
.... "I think cycling on the sidewalk is fine, with kids."
.... "There should be a law that says all children starting from age six should be educated on the rules of bicycling."
....1..... "I think the city should try to expand the system of cycle paths."
.... "Maybe some restrictions to driving downtown . . . "
.... "I'd like to bike and listen to music too, but . . . I think you should do that in a park."

6 GUESSING MEANING FROM CONTEXT

Read these sentences from the video. Guess the meanings of the underlined words.
Check (✓) your answers. Then compare with a partner.

1. More bicycles means more bicycle traffic, and that means <u>sharing the road</u>.
   - [ ] allowing others space on the road
   - [ ] expanding the road
   - [ ] decreasing the space on the road

2. Wherever bikes and cars share the road, people are going to have opinions about how they ought to <u>interact</u>.
   - [ ] think about each other
   - [ ] avoid each other
   - [ ] relate to each other

3. I think most pedestrians are <u>at ease</u> with cycling on the sidewalk.
   - [ ] comfortable
   - [ ] angry
   - [ ] excited

4. Cyclists should <u>be more aware of</u> cars, automobiles, and pedestrians.
   - [ ] be afraid of
   - [ ] pay attention to
   - [ ] try to avoid

5. Sometimes we <u>cut corners</u> in terms of moving through traffic.
   - [ ] don't stop at street corners
   - [ ] turn corners too quickly
   - [ ] try to save time

6. Montreal is <u>no exception</u>.
   - [ ] is a special situation
   - [ ] makes exceptions
   - [ ] is the same as other places

≡ Follow-up

7 FOR OR AGAINST

A You are a resident of Pleasantville, a small town about fifty kilometers from a large city. City officials have proposed replacing many of the parking places on the roads with bike lanes. Make a list of reasons for and against the bike lanes.

For	Against
would encourage cycling	would make it harder to park
....	....
....	....

B GROUP WORK Work in groups of four. Discuss the reasons **for** and **against** building the bike lanes.
Then decide whether or not to build them. Use language like this:

In my opinion . . .	That's a good point. Nevertheless, . . .	On the other hand . . .
I feel that . . .	That's an interesting idea. However, . . .	I don't think that . . .

  Interchange VRB 3 © Cambridge University Press 2012   Photocopiable

8 WHAT DID THEY SAY?

Watch the video and complete the commentaries. Then compare with a partner.

Montreal residents talk about their opinions on cycling in the city.

Sebastian: I think the city should try to .... the system of
.... paths. One thing I .... this morning
is that one .... drive .... traffic because
that's a .... Sometimes there are corners where
.... just cannot see you coming, and so you should really
try to .... driving against the ...., if possible.

*   *   *

Nitai: Cyclists should have their own bike .... and drive
towards the .... traffic .... they will be able
to better see .... the other .... cars are
doing, ... they're driving or ...., the
cyclist will have more ....

9 PASSIVE MODALS *Giving opinions on cyclists and drivers*

Read these complaints from cyclists and drivers.

Common Complaints on the Road	
Cyclists say:	**Drivers say:**
"Many drivers go much faster than the speed limit."	"Cyclists don't put lights on their bikes when riding at night."
"Sometimes drivers park in our bike lanes."	"Some cyclists don't wear bike helmets."
"Drivers don't check their rearview mirrors before opening their doors."	"Some cyclists ignore traffic signals."

What do you think about these complaints? Choose a modal from the box that shows how strongly you feel and rewrite each complaint. You can add words such as **allowed**, **required**, and **permitted.**

ought to be	**should be**	**must be**
shouldn't be	**have to be**	**mustn't be**

1. Drivers shouldn't be permitted to go faster than the speed limit. ....
2. ....
3. ....
4. ....
5. ....
6. ....

The Harlem Children's Zone

1 CULTURE

In some low-income neighborhoods in cities in the United States, public school students are struggling. They lag far behind those attending schools in higher-income neighborhoods in terms of academic success and college admission. Some experts say the following factors contribute to the difference in educational outcomes:

- the number of days students are absent from school
- the number of hours they spend watching television
- the number of pages they read for homework
- the quantity and quality of reading material in the students' homes

What kinds of educational challenges are you facing right now? Talk about some challenges you have faced in the past. Are you interested in going to college? If so, what are you thinking about studying? What is your ultimate career goal?

2 VOCABULARY Education

A Choose phrases from the box to complete the sentences.

achievement gap	✓ break the cycle	inner city	scientific data
affluent suburbs	grade level	remarkable job	statistical study

1. In order to ....*break the cycle*.... of poverty, it is necessary to improve schools.
2. Students in the .... often attend overcrowded and poorly-run schools.
3. Students who go to school in .... usually have more educational opportunities than urban students.
4. An .... occurs when one group of students performs better in school than another group.
5. In some schools, students are performing below .... , which means they're not learning as much as they should.
6. Researchers presented .... to show how well students are performing.
7. Many teachers do a .... of teaching students in difficult situations.
8. In a .... , researchers collect information to understand more about a subject.

B PAIR WORK Compare your answers. Take turns using the phrases in original sentences.

Interchange VRB 3 © Cambridge University Press 2012 Photocopiable

3 GUESS THE FACTS

Watch the first minute and a half of the video with the sound off.
Answer these questions.

1. Who are the two men?
2. What are they talking about?
3. Where do the scenes with children take place?

Watch the video

4 GET THE PICTURE

Check (✓) the items that describe the school in the video.

- ☐ It is a school for kids from the suburbs.
- ☐ It is a school for kids from the inner city.
- ☐ It is a charter school run by Geoffrey Canada.
- ☐ It is part of the public school system.
- ☐ Students are in class more often than in other schools.
- ☐ Summer vacation is longer than at most schools.
- ☐ It improves learning skills and test scores for its students.

5 WATCH FOR DETAILS

A Check (✓) **True** or **False**. Then compare with a partner.

	True	False
1. The Children's Zone covers 97 blocks in Harlem.	☐	☐
2. Geoffrey Canada doesn't want his students to go to college.	☐	☐
3. Canada grew up in Harlem.	☐	☐
4. There is one adult for every 20 children in the school.	☐	☐
5. There are 1200 children enrolled in Canada's school.	☐	☐
6. Children at Canada's school attend classes on Saturday.	☐	☐
7. One hundred percent of Canada's third graders scored at or above grade level.	☐	☐
8. Canada will know the Children's Zone has worked when they get more students.	☐	☐

B PAIR WORK Tell a partner how you would correct the false statements in part A.
Then share some more details that you remember with your partner.

6 GUESSING MEANING FROM CONTEXT

Read these sentences from the video and guess the meanings of the underlined words.
Check (✓) your answers. Then compare with a partner.

1. Geoffrey Canada may have figured out a way to close the racial achievement gap.
   - ☐ difference
   - ☐ cause
   - ☐ problem

2. Abandoned by his father, he and three brothers were raised by their mother.
   - ☐ loved
   - ☐ left forever
   - ☐ confused

3. His laboratory is a 97-block neighborhood in Harlem, which he's flooded with a wide array of social, medical, and educational services.
   - ☐ building
   - ☐ list
   - ☐ variety

4. Today, however, results are in and they are nothing short of stunning, so much so that the White House is now taking notice.
   - ☐ disappointing
   - ☐ amazing
   - ☐ normal

5. Right now, there are some twelve hundred kids enrolled from kindergarten to the tenth grade. It'll eventually expand all the way through the twelfth grade.
   - ☐ carefully
   - ☐ immediately
   - ☐ in the future

Follow-up

7 WHAT'S YOUR OPINION?

A Which features discussed in the video do you think are the most important in improving education for all students? Rank them from 1 (most important) to 6 (least important). Then add your own ideas.

.... smaller class size
.... weekend classes
.... a longer school day
.... free social and medical services
.... shorter summer vacation
.... more teachers

....
....
....

B **PAIR WORK** Take turns describing the features that are most important to you. Use sentences like these:

A: I think small classes are the best way to improve education.
B: I'm not sure. As far as I'm concerned, weekend classes are more important, because . . .

8 WHAT DID THEY SAY?

Watch the video and complete the commentaries. Then compare with a partner.

A reporter talks with Dr. Roland Fryer about the Harlem Children's Zone.

Reporter: What is the .... achievement gap?

Dr. Fryer: Black .... in our schools are not .... at

even .... the rate as white children in our schools.

The .... black seventeen-year-old ....

at the proficiency .... of the .... white

thirteen-year-old. A four-year .... in effective

.... : that's . . . that's ....

Reporter: But when Dr. Fryer .... four years' worth of

Promise Academy .... scores, he ....

something ....

Dr. Fryer: At the .... school level, he ....

the achievement .... in ....

subjects: .... and reading.

Reporter: .... eliminating the .... in elementary .... ?

Dr. Fryer: Absolutely. We've .... seen . . . we've .... seen

anything .... that.

9 COMPLEX NOUN PHRASES WITH GERUNDS

A **PAIR WORK** Interview a partner about a challenge that he or she has faced
in life, such as taking a trip, learning a new skill, or accomplishing a goal. Use five
of the questions below in your interview. Write your partner's responses below.

What was the most challenging part of . . . ?   What was the most surprising thing about . . . ?
What was one of the rewards of . . . ?   What was the most exciting thing about . . . ?
What was the most dangerous part of . . . ?   What was the scariest thing about . . . ?
What was the easiest part of . . . ?   What was the funniest thing about . . . ?

1. *The most challenging part of Anita's marathon was going up the hills.*

2. ....

3. ....

4. ....

5. ....

B **GROUP WORK** Join another pair. Explain your partner's challenge to them.

1 Dream Date

LANGUAGE SUMMARY

Topics/Functions: Dating; expressing feelings; describing personalities
Structures: Clauses containing it *with adverbial clauses*

STORY SUMMARY

The video presents a game show in which a young woman selects one of three bachelors to go on a date with her. She asks questions about their personal qualities and interests in order to make her decision.

Preview

1 CULTURE

The culture note presents information on dating in North America. If you have students who come from cultures that discourage dating or are too young to have experience with dating, have them talk about same-sex friendship instead of dates.

• Have students read the culture note silently. Then answer their questions about vocabulary or content.

• Read the questions aloud, and have students work in small groups to answer them.

• Check answers around the class.

2 VOCABULARY

In this activity, students work with key vocabulary from the video by matching an adjective with the correct description.

• Explain the task, and review the example with students.

• Have students work in pairs to complete the task. Then have pairs join together to form small groups and compare their answers.

• Check answers as a class.

> **Answers**
> 1. egotistical
> 2. easygoing
> 3. straightforward
> 4. ambitious
> 5. a good conversationalist
> 6. generous

3 GUESS THE STORY

In this activity, students prepare to watch the video by using visual information to make predictions about the video.

• Explain the task, and read the questions aloud. Direct students' attention to the photos of the three men.

• Have students work alone to guess which one of the men Elizabeth will choose.

• Check predictions around the class, but don't tell students the answer yet. Tell students they will find out if their predictions are correct in the next activity.

Watch the video

4 GET THE PICTURE

In these activities, students watch and listen to the video in order to check their predictions from Exercise 3. Then they identify things Elizabeth said, and finally they identify personality traits of the characters in the video.

A

- Explain the task, and make sure students understand they should look at their answer in Exercise 3 and check it as they watch.
- Play the entire video with the sound on as students complete the task. Ask students to raise their hands if they guessed correctly.

B

- Explain the task and read through the questions and statements with the class.
- Play the entire video with the sound on. Have students work alone to complete the task as they watch.
- Have students compare their answers with a partner. Replay the video as necessary.
- Check answers as a class.

Answers

Elizabeth said:
Describe to me your ideal date.
Tell me two things about yourself: one positive and one negative.
Finish this sentence: "I think it's disgusting when . . ."

C

- Explain the task and read through the words in the box.
- Have students work alone to complete the task. Then have them compare their answers with a partner.
- Check answers as a class.

Possible answers

1. Elizabeth: excited
2. Bachelor 1: easygoing
3. Bachelor 2: straightforward
4. Bachelor 3: egotistical

5 WATCH FOR DETAILS

In this activity, students focus on details in the video in order to correct mistakes in a summary about the bachelors.

- Explain the task, and read through the summary. Review the sample correction and make sure students understand the passage contains more errors that they need to correct.
- Have students work alone to correct as many errors as they can before watching the video.
- Play the entire video with the sound on. Have students work alone to check their predictions and complete the task.
- Have students compare their answers with a partner. Replay the video as necessary.
- Check answers as a class.

Answers

Bachelor 1 is a **writer** and a former college soccer **star** who loves playing or watching almost every kind of **sport**. Bachelor **3** is a model, who also studies **marketing**. Everyone should recognize him from his latest **running shoe** ad on **billboards** and in magazines. Bachelor **2** is the Director of Educational Programs at a **science museum**. In his free time, he enjoys **reading**, running, and **camping**. He and Elizabeth went to **high school** together.

6 WHO SAID WHAT?

In this activity, students watch and listen more closely to determine who said certain things in the video.

- Explain the task, and lead students through the chart. Have students work alone or in pairs to answer as many of the questions as they can before they watch the video again.
- Play the entire video with the sound on. Have students work alone to check their answers as they watch. Have students compare answers with a partner.
- Check answers as a class.

Answers

Bachelor 1
1. I'd be too embarrassed to tell you the truth.
7. Well, I'm pretty easygoing.

Bachelor 2
2. It really bothers me when people lie.
4. I'd take you out to a nice dinner.
5. I think I'm a pretty good friend, and reliable.
Bachelor 3
3. It's hard to split my time among so many people!
6. Actually, I'm a pretty good guy.

 Follow-up

7 ROLE PLAY

In this activity, students further develop their understanding of the video by writing additional questions Elizabeth might ask the bachelors and then role-playing *Dream Date*.

A
- Explain the task, and lead students through the statements.
- Have students work in pairs to complete the task.

B
- Explain the task, and model the example dialog. Have students work in groups of four to do the role play.
- If time permits, ask volunteers to act out their role play for the class.

 Language close-up

8 WHAT DID THEY SAY?

This cloze activity develops bottom-up listening skills by having students focus on specific language from the video.

- Explain the task. Have students work alone or in pairs to read the text and fill in as many blanks as they can before watching the video.
- Play this segment of the video with the sound on while students work alone to fill in the blanks and check their predictions. Then have students compare answers with a partner.

- Check answers as a class.
- If time permits, ask volunteers to stand up and read the text aloud.

Answers

Elizabeth: Bachelor Number 1, finish this sentence: "I **can't stand** it when . . ."

Bachelor 1: I **can't stand** it when . . . people **talk** when I'm **trying to watch** the soccer match on TV.

Elizabeth: Bachelor Number 3, finish this sentence: "I **think** it's **disgusting** when . . ."

Bachelor 3: I **think** it's **disgusting** when . . . when I go to a fancy **restaurant** and I don't get the **service** I deserve.

Elizabeth: Bachelor Number 2, finish this sentence: "It **really bothers** me when . . ."

Bachelor 2: It **really bothers** me when . . . people **argue** over unimportant things. I just think people should be less **temperamental** and more **relaxed**.

9 CLAUSES CONTAINING IT WITH ADVERBIAL CLAUSES

In these activities, students practice the grammatical focus of the unit by completing sentences about dating using clauses containing *it* with adverbial clauses.

A
- Explain the task, and lead students through the example and the phrases in the box.
- Have students work alone to complete the task. Have students compare their answers with a partner.
- Check answers as a class, and review the structure as necessary.

Possible answers

1. I can't stand it **when my date arrives late**.
2. It makes me happy **when my date sends me flowers**.
3. I like it **when my date makes me feel special**.
4. It bothers me **when my date forgets to call me**.
5. It really upsets me **when my date lies to me**.
6. It embarrasses me **when my date talks during a movie**.

B

- Explain the task, and put students into pairs to compare the statements they wrote in part A. Encourage students to ask follow-up questions.

- Ask several students to share one of their statements with the class.

2 Career moves

LANGUAGE SUMMARY

Topics/Functions: Jobs; describing personality types
Structures: Gerunds as subjects and objects

STORY SUMMARY

Jamie Fitch interviews a career counselor who talks about the relationship between personality types and different kinds of jobs.

Preview

 1 CULTURE

The culture note introduces some background information about career counseling and the relationship between personality type and career choice in order to build interest in and increase overall understanding of the video.

- Have students read the culture note about jobs silently. Then answer their questions about vocabulary or content.
- Read the questions, and have students work in small groups to answer them.
- Check answers around the class.

2 VOCABULARY

In these activities, students work with vocabulary to describe attributes of jobs, including terms that are presented in the video.

A

- Explain the task. Lead students through the words in the box, and go over the example.
- Have students work alone to complete the task. Then have students compare their answers with a partner.
- Check answers around the class.

Answers

1. independent   3. practical   5. collaborative
2. creative   4. physical   6. precise

B

- Explain the task, and model the example conversation.
- Have students work in pairs to complete the task.
- Check answers by asking volunteer pairs to share one of their conversations with the class.

3 GUESS THE STORY

In this activity, students prepare to watch the video by using visual information to make predictions about the story.

- Explain the task, and lead students through the questions.
- Play the first minute of the video (until Jamie and Ms. Auden have begun talking together) with the sound off, and tell students to watch for the answers.
- Check predictions around the class, but don't tell students the answers yet. Tell students they will find out if their predictions are correct in the next activity.

Watch the video

4 GET THE PICTURE

In the first activity, students watch and listen to check their answers from Exercise 3. In the second activity, they watch and listen for what personality types are best suited to the jobs pictured.

A

- Explain the task, and make sure students understand they should look at their answers to Exercise 3 to check them as they watch.
- Play the entire video with the sound on as students complete the task. Ask students to raise their hands if they guessed correctly.

Answers

1. The conversation is taking place in an office on a college campus.
2. The man is an interviewer, and the woman is a career counselor. They are discussing personality types that fit certain jobs.

B

- Explain the task, and lead students through the pictures.
- Play the entire video with the sound on as students complete the task.
- Have students compare their answers in pairs. Then go over answers with the class.

Answers

1. investigative
2. realistic
3. social
4. conventional

5 MAKING INFERENCES

In this activity, students focus on details in the video in order to make inferences about what happens in the video.

- Explain the task, and tell students that making an inference is like making a good guess based on what you know.
- Read through the chart and have students work alone to predict the answers before they watch.
- Play the entire video with the sound on. Have students work alone to complete the task. Then have them compare answers with a partner.
- Check answers as a class.

Answers

1. False   3. True   5. False   7. True
2. True   4. False   6. True

6 WHAT'S YOUR OPINION?

In these activities, students match people's personality types with various jobs at an ad agency.

A

- Explain the task, and lead students through the chart. Answer any questions about vocabulary.
- Have students work alone to complete the task. Have students compare their answers with a partner.
- Check answers as a class.

Possible answers

1. Bernie: accountant (likes details)
2. Fatima: manager (likes to run things)
3. Yoko: perhaps none of the above
4. Carlos: ad designer (likes creative projects)

B

- Explain the task. Then put students into small groups to complete the task.
- Ask several groups to share their ideas with the class.

Possible answers

1. Bernie: proofreader
2. Fatima: CEO
3. Yoko: researcher, corporate librarian
4. Carlos: copywriter

Follow-up

7 ARE THEY DOING THE RIGHT JOBS?

In this activity, students relate their real-world knowledge and experience to the content of the video by deciding if people they know are in the right job based on their personality type.

A

- Explain the task, and lead students through the chart and the example.

- Have students work alone to complete the task. Encourage students to provide as many details as they can.

B

- Explain the task, and put students into pairs to complete the task.
- Have pairs join together with another pair to compare answers.
- If time permits, ask selected pairs to share information with the class about one of the people they described.

Language close-up

8 WHAT DID THEY SAY?

This cloze activity develops bottom-up listening skills by having students focus on specific language from the video.

- Explain the task. Have students work alone or in pairs to read the text and fill in as many blanks as they can before watching the video.
- Play this segment of the video with the sound on while students work alone to fill in the blanks and check their predictions. Then have students compare answers with a partner.
- Check answers as a class.
- If time permits, ask for volunteers to stand up and read the text aloud.

Answers

Ms. Auden: There are six **basic** personality types: **artistic**, conventional, enterprising, investigative, realistic, and **social**. The **first** type is artistic. These **people** are **creative** and imaginative, and they **prefer** to work on one **project** at a time, rather than multi-tasking.

Jamie: What **careers** should artistic **types** pursue?

Ms. Auden: The most **important** thing for **this** type of people is being in **charge** of a **creative** project. So, **careers** to consider are landscaping, graphic **design**, web design.

Jamie: I **see**. The **next** personality type is conventional. Tell us **about** that one.

Ms. Auden: Yes. Conventional types are **practical** and orderly. They **respond** well to rules, **procedures**, schedules, **things** like that.

9 GERUNDS AS SUBJECTS AND OBJECTS

In these activities, students practice the grammatical and functional focus of the unit by using subject and object gerunds to describe jobs.

A

- Explain the task, and read through the words and phrases in the box.
- Have students work alone to complete the task. Then have students compare answers with a partner.
- Check answers as a class.

Answers

1. working with children
2. Staying in shape
3. working on weekends
4. organizing the game schedule
5. improving their skills
6. Encouraging

Job described: Children's athletic coach (e.g., soccer, baseball, etc.)

B

- Explain the task, and have students work alone to choose a job and think of the duties of that job.
- Put students into pairs to take turns describing their job duties to their partners, who try to guess the job.
- If time permits, have students change partners and repeat the exercise.

3 Common ground

LANGUAGE SUMMARY

Topics/Functions: Babysitting; asking favors
Structures: Indirect requests

STORY SUMMARY

Anne is called out of town on business on the same night she's supposed to babysit her younger sister, Megan. Anne asks her friend Rachel for help, and Rachel agrees to take care of Megan for the night. At first it seems as though they might not get along, but they find a common interest in a book from the Twilight saga. (Note: The Twilight saga is a series of novels popular with teens and adults.)

Preview

1 CULTURE

The culture note presents information about babysitting in the U.S. and Canada in the form of advice to babysitters in order to prepare students to work with the unit and build interest in the story.

- Have students read the culture note silently. Then answer their questions about vocabulary or content.
- Read the questions aloud, and have students work in small groups to answer them.
- Check answers around the class.

2 VOCABULARY

In this activity, students practice the language of requests and responses that they will hear in the video by matching requests with responses and practicing with a partner.

- Explain the task, and go over the example.
- Have students work in pairs to complete the task. Have pairs join together with another pair to compare answers.
- Check answers around the class.

Answers
1. d
2. a
3. f
4. b
5. c
6. e

3 GUESS THE STORY

In this activity, students prepare to watch the video by using visual information to make a prediction about the story.

- Explain the task, and read the question aloud.
- Play the first minute of the video with the sound off (until Anne leaves Rachel's home). Have students work alone to write their predictions. Then have them compare predictions with a partner.
- Check predictions around the class, but don't tell students the answer yet. Tell them that they will find out the answer in the next activity.

Answer
One woman is asking her friend the favor of babysitting her younger sister.

Watch the video

4 GET THE PICTURE

In these activities, students watch and listen to the video to put the events in order and then match each request with the picture that the request describes.

- Explain the task, and give students time to look at the pictures. Then have students work alone or in pairs to predict the order of the pictures before they watch the video.
- Play the entire video with the sound on. Have students check and correct their predictions as they watch. Then have them compare answers with a partner.
- Play the video again if necessary before checking answers as a class.

Answers

(from left to right)

4	3	1
5	6	2

- Explain the second part of the task, and have students work alone to write a request under the correct picture. Then have them compare answers with a partner.
- Check answers as a class.

Answers

5 Could I have something to eat?
4 Could you please turn down the volume?
1 Would you mind if she stayed with you tonight?
6 Could we watch the second movie after this one is over?
2 Can we watch them?
3 Is it OK if I watch the movie now?

5 MAKING INFERENCES

In this activity, students watch and listen more closely in order to make inferences about what happens in the video.

- Explain the task, and read through the chart. Tell students that making an inference is like making a good guess based on what you know.
- Have students work alone to predict the answers before they watch the video.
- Play the entire video with the sound on. Have students work alone to check their predictions and complete the task. Then have them compare answers with a partner.
- Check answers around the class.

Answers

1. True
2. False
3. True
4. True
5. True
6. False
7. True

WHO SAID WHAT?

In this activity, students watch and listen more closely to determine who said certain things in the video.

- Explain the task, and lead students through the chart. Have students work alone or in pairs to answer as many items as they can before watching the video again.
- Play the entire video with the sound on. Have students work alone to complete the task.
- Have students compare answers with a partner before checking answers as a class.

Answers

Anne
1. I need a big favor.
6. You two really seemed to hit it off.
Megan
2. Hey, you've got the *Twilight* movies!
4. I'm starving.
Rachel
3. How's the homework coming?
5. You've never read any of the books or seen the movies?

Follow-up

7 ROLE PLAY

In these activities, students have the chance to be creative by imagining that they are either having a big party or moving to a new home and must request help from a friend.

A

- Explain the task, and lead students through the example and the sample dialog.
- Put students into pairs to complete the task. Give students a moment to write their requests or review ways of responding to requests.
- Ask selected pairs to act out their role play for the class.

B

- Repeat the procedure in part A above.

Language close-up

8 WHAT DID THEY SAY?

This cloze activity develops bottom-up listening skills by having students focus on specific language from the video.

- Explain the task. Have students work alone or in pairs to read the text and fill in as many blanks as they can before watching the video.
- Play this segment of the video with the sound on while students work alone to fill in the blanks and check their predictions. Then have students compare answers with a partner.
- Check answers as a class.
- Ask volunteer groups to stand up and act out the conversation.

Answers

Anne: Rachel! I am so **glad** you're home. I was **wondering** if you could help me out.
Rachel: Yeah. **What's up**, Anne?
Anne: I **need** a big **favor**. My **boss** just called, and he wants me to go out of town **this afternoon** to meet with a client.

Rachel: **That's great.**
Anne: Yeah. But my **parents** are out of town, too, and my little sister, Megan, is **staying** with me. **Would you mind** if she stayed with you **tonight**? I **could** pick her up **tomorrow** by ten.
Rachel: No, I **don't mind** at all. What **time** did you want to **bring** her over?
Anne: How about **now**?

9 INDIRECT REQUESTS

In these activities, students practice the grammatical and functional focus of the unit by using indirect requests to ask favors.

A

- Explain the task, and lead students through the expressions in the box. Have students work alone to complete the task.
- Have students compare answers with a partner.
- Check answers around the class.

Answers

Anne: Would you mind **taking in the mail every day?**
Anne: Great. And could you **feed the fish**?
Anne: And let's see. I was wondering if you could **water the plants**?
Anne: Great. Oh, and I was wondering if you'd mind **walking the dog**?
Anne: Only three times a day. Anyway, one more thing. Is it OK if Megan **spends the weekend**?

B

- Explain the task, and put students into pairs. Tell pairs to brainstorm several requests to make of each other in order to complete the task.
- Have students take turns asking each other favors.
- Ask several students to share their requests with the class.

4 Around the campfire

LANGUAGE SUMMARY

Topics/Functions: Campfire stories; telling a story in the past
          Structures: Past tense verbs: past continuous, simple past, and past perfect

STORY SUMMARY

Ellen, Vanessa, and Molly are camping in the woods. Ellen is telling a scary story she heard about the campground, when the park ranger arrives and startles the young women. Have they just seen the ghost mentioned in the story?

 Preview

 CULTURE

Telling scary stories around the campfire is a popular activity in the United States and Canada. The culture note gives students some information about storytelling in North America to increase interest in the story.

- Have students read the culture note silently. Then answer their questions about vocabulary or content.
- Read the questions aloud, and have students work in pairs to answer them.
- Check answers around the class.

2 VOCABULARY

In this activity, students practice distinguishing words with similar meanings that are used in the video by matching them with a corresponding picture.

- Explain the task, and lead students through the illustrations and text below each set of pictures.
- Have students work alone to complete the task. Then have them compare answers with a partner.
- Check answers around the class.

Answers
1. surprised, freaked out
2. a mysterious situation, a scary situation
3. a hoot, a scream
4. a campground, a farm

3 GUESS THE STORY

In this activity, students prepare to watch the video by using visual information to make predictions about what happens in the story.

- Explain the task, and have students look at the pictures. Read the answer choices aloud.
- Have students work alone to complete the task. Have them compare their predictions with a partner.
- Check predictions around the class, but don't tell students the correct answers. Tell them they will find out the answers in the next activity.

 Watch the video

4 GET THE PICTURE

In these activities, students watch and listen for information to check their predictions from Exercise 3 and to decide whether statements about the story are true or false.

A

- Explain the task. Make sure students understand they should look at their answers in Exercise 3.
- Play the entire video with the sound on as students complete the task. Have students compare their answers with a partner, and replay the video as necessary.
- Check answers as a class.

> **Answers**
> She has just taken a shower.
> She is going to tell a story.
> He is greeting the girls.

B

- Explain the task, and read through the statements with the class.
- Have students work alone to predict whether the statements are true or false before watching the video again.
- Play the entire video with the sound on as students complete the task. Have students compare their answers with a partner, and replay the video as necessary.
- Have students work in pairs to correct the false statements.
- Check answers as a class.

> **Answers**
> 1. False (She heard a story at the bathhouse.)
> 2. True
> 3. True
> 4. False (His wife died in a fire.)

5 WATCH FOR DETAILS

In this activity, students watch and listen more closely in order to complete more detailed sentences about the story.

- Explain the task, and lead students through the example.
- Have students work alone or in pairs to fill in as many blanks as they can before watching the video again.

- Play the entire video with the sound on. Have students work alone to check their predictions and complete the task as they watch. Have them compare answers with a partner.
- Check answers as a class.

> **Answers**
> 1. daughter
> 2. chicken
> 3. relative
> 4. held hands
> 5. flowers/wildflowers
> 6. Dolly
> 7. the park ranger/Ted McShane

6 MAKING INFERENCES

In this activity, students focus more closely on details in the video in order to make inferences about what happens in the story.

- Explain the task, and tell students that making an inference is like making a good guess based on what you know.
- Read the statements and have students work alone to predict the answers before they watch the video again.
- Play the entire video with the sound on. Have students work alone to complete the task. Then have them compare answers with a partner.
- Check answers as a class.

> **Answers**
> 1. True
> 2. True
> 3. True
> 4. False
> 5. True
> 6. False

7 DO YOU BELIEVE THESE STORIES?

In this activity, students have the opportunity to discuss the Loch Ness Monster and Alien Big Cats, and decide if they believe in these creatures.

- Explain the task, and direct students' attention to the pictures.
- Have students read the paragraphs silently. Answer their questions about vocabulary or content. Then lead students through the example conversation.
- Put students into small groups to complete the task. Encourage groups to take notes about their discussions.
- Ask several groups to share their discussions with the class.

 Language close-up

8 WHAT DID THEY SAY?

This cloze activity develops bottom-up listening skills by having students focus on specific language from the video.

- Explain the task. Have students work alone or in pairs to read the text and fill in as many blanks as they can before watching the video.
- Play this segment of the video with the sound on while students work alone to fill in the blanks and check their predictions. Then have students compare answers with a partner.
- Check answers as a class.
- If time permits, ask groups of three students to act out the dialog for the class.

Answers

Ranger: Oh, I'm **sorry**. I didn't mean to **frighten** you ladies. I was making my **rounds** and **wanted** to see if **everything** is all right.

Molly: Yes. A park ranger, of **course**. Yes, everything's **fine**. Ellen was **telling** us a **spooky** story when you came by.

Ranger: Campfire **stories**, huh? That's **always** fun. Well, OK, then. I'll let you **get** back to it.

Vanessa: Thanks for **checking** on us. And sorry **about** the **screams**.

Ranger: That's OK. I'm **used** to it. Hey, in the **morning** you **ladies** should take a look **down** that path. There's a **field** full of wildflowers, and **they're** in bloom right now – very **pretty**.

Vanessa: Oh! That's good to **know**. We'll **do** that. Thanks.

9 PAST TENSE VERBS

In these activities, students practice the grammatical and functional focus of the unit by using three forms of past tense verbs (simple past, past continuous, and past perfect) to complete a story.

A

- Explain the task, and review the grammar of past tense verbs if necessary.
- Have students work alone to complete the task. Then have students compare their answers with a partner.
- Check answers around the class, and review the structure as necessary.

Answers

Last Saturday I **was walking** down Elm Street when I **noticed** something strange. A very fancy sports car **was sitting** in front of the entrance to the First Bank building. No one **was** in the car, but the engine **was running**. I **stopped** next to the car to take a look. It was the first time I **had seen** a car like that. Suddenly, a man with a large bag **ran** out of the bank and **jumped** into the car. He **drove** away so fast, he almost **hit** me. Then I realized: I **had witnessed** a bank robbery!

B

- Explain the task. Put students into pairs and tell them to choose a role, A or B.
- Have pairs complete the task of telling stories and asking questions. Then tell them to switch roles. Have pairs join together with another pair to take turns telling stories and asking questions.
- If time permits, ask volunteers to share their stories with the class.

5 Travel World

LANGUAGE SUMMARY

Topics/Functions: *Cross-cultural experiences; describing customs*
Structures: *Expectations – (not) expected to, (not) supposed to, (not) customary to, (not) acceptable to*

STORY SUMMARY

Chris Brooks hosts a documentary about culture shock by introducing us to different customs around the world. Three reporters in three different countries interview people about their experiences with culture shock and the different customs they encountered.

Preview

1 CULTURE

The culture note introduces the topic of culture shock and explains the three stages of culture shock in order to build interest in the topic of the video.

- Have students read the culture note silently. Then answer their questions about vocabulary or content.
- Read the questions aloud, and have students work in small groups to answer them.
- Check answers around the class.

2 VOCABULARY

In this activity, students categorize words associated with foreign travel and then try to think of additional words for each category.

- Explain the task, and lead students through the words in the box, the categories, and the example.
- Have students work alone to complete the task. Then have students compare their answers with a partner.
- Check answers as a class. Ask selected students to share the words they added to the word map.

Answers
Customs: eating a huge meal at lunch, kissing in public, shaking hands

Feelings: afraid to make a mistake, confused, surprised
Scenery: beautiful, picturesque, spectacular

Possible additional words
Customs: bowing, driving on the other side of the road, exchanging business cards
Feelings: uncertain, nervous, relaxed
Scenery: mountains, wooded, remarkable

3 GUESS THE FACTS

In this activity, students prepare to watch the video by making predictions about the causes of culture shock described in the video.

- Explain the task, and lead students through the words.
- Have students work alone to complete the task. Then have them compare answers with a partner.
- Check predictions as a class, but don't tell students the answers yet. Tell students they will find out if their predictions are correct in the next activity.

Watch the video

4 GET THE PICTURE

In the first activity, students watch and listen to check the predictions they made in Exercise 3. In the second activity, they watch and listen for information about the people interviewed in the video.

A

- Explain the task, and make sure students understand they should look at their answers to Exercise 3.
- Play the entire video with the sound on as students complete the task. Have students compare their answers with a partner before checking them as a class.

Answers

food, greetings, transportation

B

- Explain the task, and lead students through the pictures and names.
- Play the entire video with the sound on as students complete the task. Have students compare their answers with a partner before checking them as a class.

Answers

Camilla
Lives in Brazil (Rio); visited Sweden
Andrew
Is from the United States; lives in Peru
Delfino
Is from Mexico; lives in the United States

GUESSING MEANING FROM CONTEXT

5

In this activity, students use context clues to figure out the meanings of words used in the video.

- Explain the task, and lead students through the sentences, the answer choices, and the example.
- Ask students if they want to watch the video again. Have students work alone to complete the task. Then have them compare answers with a partner.
- Check answers as a class.

Answers

1. experiences in different cultures
2. pretty
3. making me uncomfortable
4. usual

WATCH FOR DETAILS

6

In this activity, students focus more closely on details in order to match the country to its custom.

- Explain the task, and lead students through the list of countries and statements.
- Have students work alone to predict as many answers as they can before watching the video again.
- Play the entire video with the sound on. Have students work alone to complete the task. Have them compare answers with a partner.
- Check answers as a class.

Answers

1. Sweden
2. Mexico
3. Brazil
4. the United States
5. Peru

WHAT'S YOUR OPINION?

7

In these activities, students personalize the information presented in the video by ranking the customs according to their own comfort level and then discussing their opinions.

A

- Explain the task, and read through the statements with the class.
- Have students work alone to complete the task.

B

- Explain the task, and read the sample language.
- Have students work in pairs to complete the task. Encourage them to give reasons for their answers.
- Ask selected pairs to share their conversations with the class.

Follow-up

8 CROSSING CULTURES

These communicative activities deepen understanding by linking the content in this unit with students' backgrounds and experiences.

A

- Explain the task, and go over the chart. Have students work alone to complete the task.

B

- Explain the task. Put students into pairs to complete the task.
- Ask selected pairs to share their customs with the class.

Language close-up

9 WHAT DID HE SAY?

This cloze activity develops bottom-up listening skills by having students focus on specific language from the video.

- Explain the task. Have students work alone or in pairs to read the text and fill in as many blanks as they can before watching the video.
- Play this segment of the video with the sound on while students work alone to fill in the blanks and check their predictions. Then have students compare answers with a partner.
- Check answers as a class.
- If time permits, ask for volunteers to read the passage aloud.

Answers

Hi. I'm Chris Brooks. **Welcome** to *Travel World*. Have you ever **traveled** to a **country** with a **completely** different **culture**? If you have, you **probably** know what "**culture shock**" is. It's a feeling of **confusion** you get from **suddenly** being in a new **environment**. The **traditions** and **customs** may seem **strange**. **Expectations** are different. You don't know exactly what you're **supposed to** do. You may **even** be a little **bit afraid** of making a **mistake**. In **time**, you get **used to** everything. But **when** you get **home**, you often have some **interesting** and perhaps **humorous** stories to **tell** about your **cross-cultural** experiences.

10 EXPECTATIONS

In these activities, students practice the grammatical and functional focus of the unit by completing sentences that express expectations about customs.

A

- Explain the task, and model the example.
- Have students work alone to complete the task.

B

- Put students in pairs to compare their answers from part A.
- Check answers as a class, and review as needed.

Answers

1. traditional
2. expected
3. customary
4. supposed
5. tradition
6. custom
7. expectations
8. suppose

6 What's the problem?

LANGUAGE SUMMARY

Topics/Functions: Hotel complaints; describing problems; making complaints
Structures: Need *with passive infinitives and gerunds*

STORY SUMMARY

A couple goes to a quaint hotel hoping to enjoy a relaxing weekend. When they get to their room, however, they discover many problems such as a broken heater and no running water. Unfortunately, the hotel employee seems incapable of fixing anything, and the couple decides to leave.

Preview

 1 CULTURE

The culture note presents background information about a bed and breakfast in the United States. B&Bs are often historic homes that have been remodeled to function as an inn. This is probably the kind of place Ed and Michelle hoped they were going to visit in the video.

- Have students read the culture note silently. Then answer their questions about vocabulary or content.
- Read the questions aloud, and have students work in small groups to answer them.
- Check answers around the class.

 2 VOCABULARY

In this activity, students work with key vocabulary to describe problems, including some they will see in the video.

- Explain the task, and lead students through the words in the box and the example.
- Have students work alone to complete the sentences. Then have them compare answers with a partner.
- Check answers as a class.

Answers

1. dirty	5. broken
2. peeling	6. stuck
3. stained	7. fixed
4. scratched	8. cracked

- Explain the task, and give students time to look at the pictures.
- Have students work alone to match a sentence to a picture. Then have them compare answers with a partner.
- Check answers as a class.

Answers

(from left to right)

6	4	2	1
5	3	8	7

3 GUESS THE STORY

In this activity, students prepare to watch the video by using visual information to make predictions about what happens in the story.

- Explain the task, and lead students through the pictures and answer choices.
- Have students work alone to complete the task. Then have them compare answers with a partner.
- Check predictions around the class, but don't tell students the answers yet. Tell students they will find out if their predictions are correct in the next activity.

Answers
1. The older man is giving instructions.
2. The couple is here to relax.
3. The man is calling the front desk.

 ## Watch the video

 ## 4 GET THE PICTURE

In this activity, students watch and listen to the video to identify problems with Ed and Michelle's hotel room.

- Explain the task, and lead students through the chart.
- Play the entire video with the sound on, and have students check off the answers as they watch.
- Have students compare answers with a partner. Replay the video if needed before checking answers with the class.

Answers

1. broken, stuck	4. stuck
2. peeling	5. dirty
3. scratched	

5 WATCH FOR DETAILS

In this activity, students focus more closely on details to identify descriptions of the characters in the video.

- Explain the task. Read through the statements and have students fill in as many blanks as they can before watching the video again.
- Play the entire video with the sound on. Have students work alone to complete the task. Then have them compare answers with a partner.
- Check answers as a class.

Answers

1. George	5. Ed
2. Michelle	6. Norman
3. Ed	7. Michelle
4. Norman	8. George

 ## 6 WHAT'S YOUR OPINION?

In this activity, students give their opinions about what happened in the story, and they relate the problems to a similar situation in their own lives.

- Explain the task, and read the questions aloud. Make sure students understand they should answer according to their own opinions and experiences.
- Have students work in pairs to complete the task. Encourage students to take notes as they talk.
- Have pairs join together with another pair to compare opinions and experiences.
- Ask selected students to share their opinions and experiences with the class. Encourage students to give reasons for their opinions.

Follow-up

7 ROLE PLAY

In these activities, students extend the language of describing problems to a restaurant scene. They then role-play the problems and solutions.

A

- Explain the task, and give students time to look at the picture.
- Have students work in pairs to complete the task.
- Check answers as a class.

Possible answers

The plate is cracked.
The tablecloth is dirty and torn.
The food on the waiter's tray is burned.
The water glass is broken.
The waiter's jacket is dirty.
The ceiling is leaking.
The window glass is cracked.
The table has bugs crawling on it.
The chandelier is broken.
The soup has a fly in it.
The menu has a hole in it.
The children are noisy.
The restaurant has mice.

B

- Explain the task, and read through the sample conversation.
- Have pairs join together with another pair to form groups of four. Have groups perform the role play for as many problems as they can.
- Call on selected groups to perform one of their role plays for the class.

 Language close-up

8 WHAT DID THEY SAY?

This cloze activity develops bottom-up listening skills by having students complete part of the conversation from the video.

- Explain the task. Have students work alone or in pairs to read the text and fill in as many blanks as they can before watching the video.
- Play this segment of the video with the sound on while students work alone to fill in the blanks and check their predictions. Then have students compare answers with a partner.
- Check answers as a class.
- If time permits, ask for volunteers to stand up and act out the conversation.

Answers

Norman: Hi. What's the **problem**?
Michelle: Oh, it's **cold**.
Norman: **Turn up** the heat.
    Ed: The heat **doesn't work**.
Norman: Well, what's **wrong** with it?
Michelle: The dial's **broken**. It came off in my **hand**.
Norman: That should **do** it.
    Ed: **We'll see**. That window needs **fixing**, too. It's **stuck** and it's letting the **cold** air in.
Norman: That should **do** it.
Michelle: **Thanks**?
Norman: You're **welcome**.

9 NEED *WITH PASSIVE INFINITIVES AND GERUNDS*

In these activities, students practice the grammatical and functional focus of the unit by describing problems using passive infinitives and gerunds. Then they personalize the activity by talking about problems in their own environment.

A

- Explain the task, and read Norman's list aloud. Answer any vocabulary questions.
- Review the example, and have students work alone to complete the task. Then put students into pairs to compare answers.
- Check answers as a class, and review the structure as necessary.

Possible answers

1. The heat needs adjusting. / The heat needs to be adjusted.
2. The wastebasket needs emptying. / The wastebasket needs to be emptied.
3. The chair needs repairing. / The chair needs to be repaired.
   or
   The chair needs fixing. / The chair needs to be fixed.
4. The hair dryer needs fixing. / The hair dryer needs to be fixed.
   or
   The hair dryer needs repairing. / The hair dryer needs to be repaired.
5. The rooms need cleaning. / The rooms need to be cleaned.
6. The floors need washing. / The floors need to be washed.

B

- Explain the task. Be sure to tell students that it's OK to make up chores that need to be done if they have trouble thinking of things.
- Have students work alone to complete the task. Then put students into pairs to share their sentences.
- Have selected students share one of their sentences with the class.

7 Endangered islands

LANGUAGE SUMMARY

Topics/Functions: Climate change; describing environmental problems
Structures: The passive and prepositions of cause

STORY SUMMARY

This news report from the BBC focuses on climate change as it impacts the island nation of Tuvalu in the South Pacific – the islands of this country are disappearing because of changes in sea level. The reporter talks to residents and climate experts to present information about the effects of climate change.

☰ Preview

1 CULTURE

The culture note prepares students to work with the video by introducing the topic of climate change and presents some information about the effects of climate change in order to build interest in and increase overall understanding of the video.

- Have students read the culture note silently. Then answer their questions about vocabulary or content.
- Read the questions aloud, and have students work in small groups to answer them.
- Check answers around the class.

2 VOCABULARY

In this activity, students become familiar with some vocabulary used in the video by completing sentences using the target words.

- Explain the task, lead students through the sentences, and review the example.
- Have students work alone to complete the task. Have students compare answers with a partner.
- Check answers as a class.

Answers

1. catastrophic event
2. technological fix
3. coastal areas
4. climate panel
5. global warming
6. high tide

3 GUESS THE FACTS

In this activity, students prepare to watch the video by using visual information to make predictions about the story.

- Explain the task, and lead students through the answer choices.
- Play the first two minutes of the video with the sound off (before the child swings in the hammock). Have students work alone to make their predictions. Then have students compare their predictions with a partner.
- Check predictions around the class, but don't tell students the answers yet. Tell students they will find out if their predictions are correct in the next activity.

Watch the video

 GET THE PICTURE

In the first activity, students watch and listen to check their answers from Exercise 3. In the second activity, they watch and listen in order to identify threats faced by the people of Tuvalu.

A

- Explain the task, and make sure students understand they should look at their answers to Exercise 3, and check them as they watch.
- Play the entire video with the sound on as students complete the task. Have students compare their answers with a partner, and replay the video as necessary.
- Check answers as a class.

> **Answers**
> flooding, high tides, strong winds

B

- Explain the task, and have students look at the pictures as you lead them through the statements.
- Play the entire video with the sound on as students complete the task. Have students compare their answers with a partner, and replay the video as necessary.
- Check answers as a class.

> **Answers**
> (from left to right)
> 2 4 1 3

 WATCH FOR DETAILS

In this activity, students focus more closely on details in order to complete sentences about Tuvalu.

- Explain the task, and lead students through the statements. Answer any vocabulary questions as they arise. Have students work alone or in pairs to fill in as many blanks as they can before watching the video.

- Play the entire video with the sound on. Have students work alone to complete the task. Have them compare answers with a partner.
- Check answers as a class.

> **Answers**
> 1. salty
> 2. 15
> 3. five to 10
> 4. two and a half
> 5. four and a half
> 6. 50
> 7. 11,000

 GUESSING MEANING FROM CONTEXT

In this activity, students use context clues to figure out the meanings of words used in the video.

- Explain the task, and read the statements and answer choices aloud.
- Have students work alone to complete the task. Then put students into pairs to compare answers.
- Check answers as a class.

> **Answers**
> 1. easily damaged
> 2. rises suddenly
> 3. terrible
> 4. measured
> 5. steps

 Follow-up

 FOR OR AGAINST

In these communicative activities, students practice giving opinions for and against providing assistance to the nation of Tuvalu.

A

- Explain the task, and direct students' attention to the chart.
- Have students work in pairs to complete the task.

B

- Explain the task, and read the example language.
- Have students work in groups of four to discuss their reasons for or against helping the country of Tuvalu. Encourage students to come to a decision.
- Ask a volunteer from each group to explain their decision and how they reached it.

Language close-up

8 WHAT DID HE SAY?

This cloze activity develops bottom-up listening skills by having students focus on specific language from the video.

- Explain the task. Have students work alone or in pairs to read the text and fill in as many blanks as they can before watching the video.
- Play this segment of the video with the sound on while students work alone to fill in the blanks and check their predictions. Then have students compare answers with a partner.
- Check answers as a class.
- If time permits, ask for volunteers to stand up and read the passage aloud.

Answers

For the children of Tuvalu, the **floods** are fun. But for them to **lead** their **lives** on these islands will require **massive** international **support**. And with **just** 11,000 people here, will the **outside** world think it's **worth** it? Now, of course, Tuvalu does get some **aid**, but not **nearly** enough to keep the **rising** sea at bay. So the **international** community **faces** very soon a difficult **choice** of **whether** to draw a line between **those** who get **saved** and those who don't. And in the **meantime**, people here are getting ready for **another** king tide. Right now it's **low**; it's due to get very **high** in about eight hours' time.

9 THE PASSIVE

This activity has students work with both the topic and the grammatical focus of the unit by using the passive to make sentences about environmental problems and solutions.

- Explain the task, and lead students through the example and sentences.
- Have students work alone to complete the task. Put students into pairs to compare answers.
- Check answers as a class, and review the structure as necessary.

Answers

1. Some of Tuvalu's coastal areas are being washed out because of king tides.
2. Most of the plant life is being killed off due to salty seawater.
3. The changes in sea level on Tuvalu are monitored by an Australian system.
4. Many coastal areas will be covered in five to ten years as a result of rising sea levels.
5. A global fund must be set up by the international community to save Tuvalu.

8 Tango!

LANGUAGE SUMMARY

Topics/Functions: Tango dancing; talking about learning methods
        Structures: Gerunds and infinitives; would rather and would prefer

STORY SUMMARY

In this documentary, Kevin Kaine speaks with tango dancers to find out why tango is popular, how they learned to dance, and advice they have for others who would like to learn. The video was filmed at the Weeks Bridge in Cambridge, Massachusetts.

≡ Preview

1 CULTURE

The culture note builds interest in the topic by giving some background information about the history of tango dancing and having students think about why people like to dance.

- Have students read the culture note silently. Then answer their questions about vocabulary or content.
- Read the questions aloud, and have students work in small groups to answer them.
- Check answers around the class.

2 VOCABULARY

In these activities, students practice vocabulary for talking about learning by matching verb phrases to their corresponding words or phrases, and using the phrases to complete sentences.

A

- Explain the task, and lead students through the lists and the example.
- Have students work in pairs to complete the task. Have pairs join together to check answers in small groups.
- Check answers as a class.

Answers
1. decide to take lessons
2. earn a diploma
3. brush up on my skills
4. learn how to ski
5. practice hitting the ball
6. take classes

B

- Explain the task, and lead students through the example. Have students work individually to complete the task. Then have them compare answers with a partner.
- Check answers as a class.

Answers
1. decide to take lessons
2. practice hitting the ball
3. brush up on my skills
4. take classes
5. earned a diploma
6. learn how to ski

3 GUESS THE FACTS

In this activity, students make predictions about the reasons for tango dancing's popularity and how people learn or improve their tango dancing.

- Explain the task, and read the questions aloud.

- Have students work individually to complete the task. Have them compare their predictions with a partner.
- Check answers as a class, but don't tell students the correct answers. Tell students they will find out the answers in Exercises 4 and 5.

 Watch the video

 4 GET THE PICTURE

In this activity, students watch and listen to identify the reasons people give for tango dancing's popularity.

- Explain the task, and lead students through the statements. Ask students if any of the statements match their predictions in Exercise 3.
- Play the entire video with the sound on. Have students complete the task as they watch. Have students compare answers with a partner.
- Check answers with the class.

Answers

They're just interested in dancing.
They want to keep fit and have fun.
The tango is exotic and challenging.
The tango has a great rhythm.

5 WATCH FOR DETAILS

In this activity, students focus more closely on the details in the video in order to answer more detailed questions about what people in the video say.

- Explain the task, and lead students through the statements.
- Play the video with the sound on. Have students complete the task as they watch.
- Ask students if they want to watch the video again. Then have students compare answers with a partner.
- Check answers around the class.

Answers

1. By going to a tango club.
2. By practicing hard.
3. By practicing with a guy.
4. By starting with group classes or private classes.
5. By taking the initiative and taking a class.

 6 WHAT'S YOUR OPINION?

In these activities, students personalize the information in the video by talking about personal qualities that are important for learning how to dance or do other activities.

A

- Explain the task, and lead students through the list. Answer any vocabulary questions.
- Have students work alone to complete the task.

B

- Explain the task, and lead students through the activities.
- Have students work in pairs to complete the task.

 Follow-up

7 ADVICE TO LEARNERS

In these activities, students extend the topic of the unit by talking about ways people could learn an activity.

A

- Explain the task, and have students work alone to complete the task.

B

- Explain the task, and read the example language.
- Put students into groups of three or four to complete the task. Have students take turns talking about their activities and asking questions.
- If time permits, ask volunteers to share their ideas for learning activities with the class.

Language close-up

8 WHAT DID THEY SAY?

This cloze activity develops bottom-up listening skills by having students focus on specific language from the video.

- Explain the task. Have students work alone or in pairs to read the text and fill in as many blanks as they can before watching the video.
- Play this segment of the video with the sound on while students work alone to fill in the blanks and check their predictions. Then have students compare answers with a partner.
- Check answers as a class.
- If time permits, ask pairs to stand up and act out the conversation for the class.

Answers

Kevin: Why do you think tango is so **popular**?
Uche: I think tango is **popular** because it's very **exotic** and it's also very **challenging** for people, and once people **learn** something that they find **challenging** and it's very **exotic**, I think they **feel** very rewarded.
Kevin: What do you **recommend** for people who **want** to learn tango?
Uche: I would recommend starting with **group** classes or **private** classes.
Kevin: And **after** you've learned the **basics** of tango, what's a good way to **improve** your moves?
Uche: By going out **dancing** with the people that you've **taken** the **lessons** with, **practicing** at home, listening to the **music**, just feeling very **comfortable** with the music, and then **going out** dancing again.

9 GERUNDS AND INFINITIVES

In these activities, students practice the grammatical and functional focus of the unit by using gerund or infinitive phrases to talk about preferences.

A

- Explain the task, and go over the example.
- Have students work alone to complete the task. Then put students into pairs to compare answers.
- Check answers as a class.

Answers

1. Would you prefer to earn a degree or learn for fun?
2. Would you rather learn English in Australia or in Canada?
3. Would you prefer to learn how to cook or how to dance the tango?
4. Would you rather brush up on skills you already have or learn something new?
5. Would you rather read English magazines or English novels?
6. Would you prefer to study in the morning or at night?

B

- Explain the task, and have students work in groups of four or five to complete the task.
- Ask selected students to share one or two pieces of information they learned about their classmates with the class.

9 Stressed out

LANGUAGE SUMMARY

Topics/Functions: Stress; making suggestions
Structures: Making suggestions with gerunds, infinitives, base-form verbs, and negative questions

STORY SUMMARY

Carmen is complaining to her co-worker Hugo about how stressed she feels. He offers suggestions, but Carmen says she's already tried them and they didn't work, except for hypnotherapy, which works too well.

Preview

1 CULTURE

The culture note introduces and builds interest in the topic by providing some background information about stress and its effects.

- Have students read the culture note silently. Then answer their questions about vocabulary or content.
- Read the questions aloud, and have students work in pairs or small groups to answer them.
- Check answers around the class.

2 VOCABULARY

In this activity, students practice using different idiomatic expressions related to stress that are used in the video.

- Explain the task, and lead students through the expressions in the box and the example. Answer any questions students may have.
- Have students work alone to complete the task.
- Check answers as a class.

> **Answers**
> Last year, I felt completely **stressed out** by my job. Every day it seemed like I was **under pressure** from my boss. My stomach was **in knots** all the time. I used to **blow off steam** by complaining to my co-workers, but that only made them feel stressed, too! Someone in my

office said I should **get some exercise**, but I felt too tired to go. Finally, my boss suggested, "Why don't you **take some time off** and go to a health spa for a few days? It'll be **very relaxing.**" It turned out to be just **what I needed**! When I got back, I felt calm and ready to handle anything.

3 GUESS THE STORY

In this activity, students prepare to watch the video by using visual information to make predictions about people in the video.

- Explain the task, and read the questions aloud.
- Play the first minute of the video with the sound off (until Carmen holds up the skate). Have students work alone to write their predictions. Then have students compare their predictions with a partner.
- Check predictions around the class, but don't tell students the answers yet. Tell students they will find out if their predictions are correct in the next activity. [The woman feels stressed; the man is giving her suggestions about how to relax.]

Watch the video

4 GET THE PICTURE

In this activity, students watch and listen to the video to identify the activities Hugo suggests to Carmen.

A

- Explain the task, and lead students through the illustrations.
- Play the entire video with the sound on. Have students check off the answers as they watch.
- Have students compare answers in pairs, and replay the video as necessary.
- Check answers around the class.

> **Answers**
>
> *(from left to right)*
> aromatherapy, dance lessons, hypnotherapy
> taking a vacation, yoga

B

- Explain the task, and put students into pairs to complete the task.
- Ask selected pairs to share their answers with the class.

5 WATCH FOR DETAILS

In this activity, students focus more closely on details to determine why Carmen didn't like Hugo's suggestions.

- Explain the task, and lead students through the statements.
- Play the entire video with the sound on. Have students complete the task as they watch.
- Have students compare their answers with a partner before checking them as a class.

> **Answers**
>
> 1. Her skate broke.
> 2. She got hurt.
> 3. It twisted her in knots.
> 4. It worked too well.
> 5. She's allergic to perfumes.

6 WHAT'S YOUR OPINION?

In these activities, students use what they've learned in the video to give reasons why Carmen might reject some activities. They then role-play

Hugo giving Carmen more suggestions for coping with stress.

A

- Explain the task, and lead students through the example and activities. Answer any vocabulary questions.
- Put students into pairs to complete the task. Have pairs join together with another pair to compare reasons.

B

- Explain the task, and read the example dialog. Have pairs do the role play, and have them switch roles.
- If time permits, ask selected pairs to act out their role play for the class.

Follow-up

7 HOW STRESSED ARE YOU?

In the first activity, students personalize the topic by discussing how much stress they feel in certain situations. In the second activity, they survey the class about the same situations.

A

- Explain the task, lead students through the chart, and go over the sample dialog.
- Have students work alone to add one more idea to the chart and to check their answers. Put students into pairs to complete the task.
- If time permits, ask selected pairs to share their answers with the class.

B

- Explain the task. Have students move about the room to ask classmates about stress and check their answers in the chart.
- Ask selected students to share their answers with the class.

 Language close-up

8 *WHAT DID THEY SAY?*

This cloze activity develops bottom-up listening skills by having students complete part of a conversation from the video.

- Explain the task. Have students work alone or in pairs to read the text and fill in as many blanks as they can before watching the video.
- Play this segment of the video with the sound on while students work alone to fill in the blanks and check their predictions. Then have students compare answers with a partner.
- Check answers as a class.
- If time permits, ask for volunteer pairs to stand up and act out the conversation for the class.

> **Answers**
>
> Hugo: There's always **hypnotherapy**.
> Carmen: I've tried that, too. Now, **every** time I **hear** the word "ocean," it's supposed to **relax** me. Oh, and it **works**! The other day, I was in a **meeting**. Someone **started** talking about the **environmental** problems in the world's **oceans**. People said the **word** "ocean" so many times, I **fell asleep**.
> Hugo: Oh, yeah. I **heard** about that. That must've been **embarrassing**.
> Carmen: Now half the **office** knows. See what I mean? I **need** to get the hypnotherapy **reversed**.
> Hugo: I have an idea. You could **try** aromatherapy.
> Carmen: **What's that?**
> Hugo: It's **like** a massage, but they **rub** your skin **with** scented oils.

9 *SUGGESTIONS*

In these activities, students practice the grammatical and functional focus of the unit by creating, making, and responding to suggestions.

A

- Explain the task, and lead students through the expressions and the sentences.
- Have students work alone to complete the task. Then put students into pairs to compare answers.
- Ask volunteers to share their answers with the class.

> **Possible answers**
>
> 1. Have you thought about listening to Spanish podcasts while you're doing something else?
> 2. It might be a good idea not to answer your phone.
> 3. Why don't you reschedule your vacation?
> 4. What about going to a museum?
> 5. One thing you could do is to start reading earlier.

B

- Explain the task, and have students work alone to write two problems.
- Put students into pairs to complete the task.
- If time permits, ask selected students to share their sentences with the class.

10 The Virtual Office

LANGUAGE SUMMARY

Topics/Functions: The workplace; comparing old and new ways of doing things

Structures: Predicting the future with will

STORY SUMMARY

This news report is about the workplace of today and possibilities for the future of telecommuting and online meetings to create the virtual office. The reporter talks to several employees and company directors to discuss how technology is changing the workplace and how people work.

☰ Preview

1 CULTURE

The culture note introduces and builds interest in the topic of the video by presenting some information about how technology is changing not only how people work but also where they work and interact with colleagues.

- Have students read the culture note silently. Then answer their questions about vocabulary or content.
- Read the questions aloud, and have students work in small groups to answer them.
- Check answers around the class.

2 VOCABULARY

In this activity, students work with key vocabulary related to the workplace, including terms used in the video.

- Explain the task, lead students through the words and phrases in the box, and have them look at the pictures. Review the example.
- Have students work alone to complete the task. Then have students compare answers with a partner.
- Check answers as a class.

Answers

1. workspace
2. corporate headquarters
3. kiosk
4. commute
5. cyberspace
6. meeting

3 GUESS THE FACTS

In this activity, students prepare to watch the video by making predictions about one of the facts presented in the video.

- Explain the task, and have students work alone to write their prediction.
- Ask selected students to share their prediction with the class. Don't tell students the answer yet. Tell them they will find out if their predictions are correct in the next activity.

☰ Watch the video

4 GET THE PICTURE

In these activities, students watch and listen to the video in order to check their predictions from Exercise 3 and to decide if statements about the video are true or false.

A

- Explain the task, and make sure students understand they should look at their predictions in Exercise 3.

- Play the entire video with the sound on. Have students work alone to check their predictions as they watch.
- Check answers around the class. Ask students to raise their hands if their prediction was correct.

Answer
42%

B

- Explain the task, and have students work alone to answer as many questions as they can before they watch the video again.
- Play the entire video with the sound on. Have students work alone to check their predictions and complete the task as they watch. Have students compare answers with a partner.
- Check answers around the class.

Answers
1. False (IBM has 350,000 employees.)
2. True
3. False (The CEO doesn't have an office [with his name on the door].)
4. True
5. False (Crayon's workers rarely meet in the physical world.)
6. False (Betsey Stark met Crayon's CEO in cyberspace/online/in the virtual boardroom.)

5 MAKING INFERENCES

In this activity, students use information they learned from the video to make inferences about the people and companies featured.

- Explain the task, and lead students through the statements.
- Have students work alone to predict as many answers as they can before watching the video again.
- Play the entire video with the sound on, and have students work alone to check their predictions and make corrections as they watch. Have students compare answers with a partner.
- Check answers as a class.

Answers
1. False	3. False	5. True
2. True	4. False	6. False

6 WATCH FOR DETAILS

In this activity, students watch and listen more closely to determine whether certain statements were made in the video.

- Explain the task, and review the statements.
- Have students work alone to answer as many questions as they can before watching the video again.
- Play the entire video with the sound on, and have students check and revise their answers as they watch. Give students time to write their own idea.
- Check answers with the class. Ask selected students to share the idea they added to the chart.

Answers
1. Meeting in cyberspace
3. Reserving a workspace only when you need it
4. Bringing people together, no matter where they are in the world
6. Having a virtual office party

 Follow-up

7 CREATE YOUR OWN VIRTUAL OFFICE

In these activities, students work with the content of the unit by choosing a job where they would work in a non-traditional workplace and creating specifications for the job including communication with colleagues.

A

- Explain the task, and lead students through the chart.
- Have students work individually to complete the task. You may want to brainstorm ideas as a class to help students get started.

B

- Explain the task, and read the example dialog.
- Put students into pairs to complete the task.
- Have selected students share their ideas with the class.

 Language close-up

 WHAT DID THEY SAY?

This cloze activity develops bottom-up listening skills by having students focus on specific language from the video.

- Explain the task. Have students work alone or in pairs to read the text and fill in as many blanks as they can before watching the video.
- Play this segment of the video with the sound on while students work alone to fill in the blanks and check their predictions. Then have students compare answers with a partner.
- Check answers as a class.

> **Answers**
>
> Anchor: Finally from us, the virtual office. For better or **worse**, technology and **globalization** are creating startling **changes** in what it **means** to be **"on the job."** Betsey Stark is tracking the **new** order of **business** and **tonight** begins our series, "The **Future** of Work."
>
> Reporter: Imagine a work **world** with no commute, no corporate **headquarters**, maybe no **office** in the **physical** world at all. For Bob Flavin, Janet Hoffman, and Joseph Jaffe, the **future** is **already** here.
>
> Bob Flavin: These days we **do** so **much** stuff by **teleconferences** and things, um, that it **doesn't matter** where you **are**.

9 PAST, PRESENT, AND FUTURE

In these activities, students practice the functional and grammatical focus of the unit by completing sentences with the correct verb form to refer to the past, present, or future.

A

- Explain the task, and lead students through the sentences and the example.
- Have students work alone to complete the task. Then put students into pairs to compare answers with a partner.
- Check answers as a class.

> **Answers**
>
> 1. **In** the 1960s, people listened to music on record players. Nowadays, people mostly **use** MP3 players. Some experts believe that people in the future **will listen** to music through chips in their brains.
> 2. **Since** the Middle Ages, most people have lived in rural areas and towns. However, this trend **has changed**. In fact, most people now **live** in cities.
> 3. **For** many years, people didn't spend time on computers and mobile devices. Now, of course, they **are** common. Some experts think that in the next few years, most people **will spend** almost 60 hours a week on electronic devices!

B

- Explain the task, and read the example.
- Put students into pairs to complete the task. Then have pairs get together with another pair to compare sentences.
- If time permits, ask selected pairs to share one of their sentences with the class.

> **Possible answers**
>
> 1. In 2050, people will live longer than they do now.
> 2. In 1900, the lifespan was shorter than it is now.
> 3. Now, people don't live as long as they will in 2050.

11 Live and learn

LANGUAGE SUMMARY

Topics/Functions: Embarrassing moments; talking about past mistakes
Structures: should have/shouldn't have + past participle; if clauses + past perfect

STORY SUMMARY

Jamie Fitch asks several people about an embarrassing moment in their lives. The guests describe what happened, what they did, and what they should or shouldn't have done instead.

📋 Preview

1 CULTURE

The culture note presents some interesting background information about embarrassing moments, regrets, and how we deal with them in order to build interest in and increase understanding of the video.

- Have students read the culture note silently. Then answer their questions about vocabulary or content.
- Read the questions aloud, and have students work in pairs or small groups to answer them.
- Check answers around the class.

2 VOCABULARY

In these activities, students first categorize vocabulary associated with events and images they will see in the video, and think of additional words to categorize. They then talk about their own mistakes and how it made them feel.

A

- Explain the task, and lead students through the words in the box, the chart, and the example.
- Have students work alone to complete the task. Then put students into pairs to compare answers.
- Check answers as a class.

Answers

Events: conference, meeting, performance
Types of businesses: advertising agency, technology company, theater
Feelings: embarrassed, spellbound, unprofessional

B

- Explain the task, and read the questions aloud.
- Have students work in pairs to complete the task. Then have pairs get together with another pair to compare answers.

3 GUESS THE STORY

In this activity, students prepare to watch the video by using visual information to make predictions about what happens in the video.

- Explain the task, and read the question aloud.
- Play the first minute of the video with the sound off (until Jamie begins talking for his second interview), and tell students to watch for the answer.
- Have students work alone to complete the task. Then have them compare their prediction with a partner. Don't tell students the answer yet. Tell them they will find out the answer in the next activity.

Answer

The interviewer is asking the woman to describe an embarrassing moment from her life.

 Watch the video

 GET THE PICTURE

In this activity, students watch and listen to the video to find out general information about the people interviewed.

- Explain the task, and direct students' attention to the photos.
- Play the entire video with the sound on. Have students work alone to complete the task as they watch.
- Have students compare their answers with a partner, and replay the video as necessary. Then check answers around the class.

Answers

	Where	Other (possible answers)
Amber:	an advertising agency	was meeting with an important client looked like she was still in college
Evan:	a friend's house	broke a vase didn't tell anyone
Alexis:	a theater	cell phone rang loudly everyone was staring at her

 WATCH FOR DETAILS

In this activity, students focus more closely on details in the video in order to determine if statements about what happened in the story are true or false.

- Explain the task, and lead students through the statements. Have students work alone to answer as many questions as they can before watching the video again.
- Play the entire video with the sound on. Have students complete the task as they watch. Give them a moment to correct the false statements.

- Have students compare their answers with a partner before checking answers as a class.

Answers

1. False (She had finished with college./She worked for an advertising agency.)
2. False (She was embarrassed in a meeting.)
3. True
4. False (He was attending a conference.)
5. True
6. False (He broke a vase.)
7. True
8. False (It rang very loudly.)

 MAKING INFERENCES

In this activity, students watch and listen more closely in order to make inferences about what happens in the video.

- Explain the task, and tell students that making an inference is like making a good guess based on what you know. Lead students through the chart.
- Have students work alone to predict the answers to as many questions as they can before watching the video again.
- Play the entire video with the sound on. Have students work alone to check their predictions and complete the task as they watch. Then have students compare their answers with a partner.
- Check answers as a class.

Answers

1. False	4. False
2. False	5. True
3. True	6. False

 Follow-up

 I SHOULD HAVE . . .

In this activity, students personalize the content of the unit by talking about embarrassing situations from their own lives.

A

- Explain the task, and lead students through the examples in the chart.
- Have students work alone to complete the task. Tell students they can make up embarrassing situations if they'd rather not share personal information.

B

- Explain the task, and put students into pairs to complete the task.
- Ask selected pairs to share one of their situations and solutions with the class.

 Language close-up

8 WHAT DID HE SAY?

This cloze activity develops bottom-up listening skills by having students focus on specific language from the video.

- Explain the task. Have students work alone or in pairs to read the text and fill in as many blanks as they can before watching the video.
- Play this segment of the video with the sound on while students work alone to fill in the blanks and check their predictions. Then have students compare answers with a partner by reading the text aloud.
- Check answers as a class.
- If time permits, ask for volunteers to stand up and read the text for the class.

Answers

I was attending a **conference** out of town and **staying** with an old friend, Ed, and his **family**.... The first morning, I **overslept**. I was rushing to leave the **house** when I knocked over a **vase** and **broke** it. No one was awake yet, and I was **in a hurry**, so I just threw away the **pieces**. By the time I **had cleaned** it up, I was really **late**, so I left. I **should have called** Ed and told him about it, but, honestly, I **forgot**. That night, when I got back to the **house**, Ed and his wife, Michelle, were having an **argument** with their son, Ben. They thought Ben **had broken** the vase and then tried to **hide** it.

9 PAST CONDITIONALS

In these activities, students practice the functional and grammatical focus of the unit by using past conditionals to discuss regrets and speculations about the past.

A

- Explain the task, and go over the example.
- Have students work alone to complete the task. Then have students compare answers with a partner.
- Check answers around the class, and review the structure as necessary.

Answers

1. If I had gone to bed early, I wouldn't have fallen asleep during the test.
2. If she hadn't taken summer classes, she wouldn't have graduated early.
3. If he had known the answer, he wouldn't have been embarrassed.
4. If they hadn't brought a map, they would have gotten lost.
5. If you had heard the announcement, you wouldn't have missed your train.
6. If we hadn't bought a new car, we would have had money for a vacation.

B

- Explain the task, and read the situations.
- Have students work in groups of three or four to complete the task.
- Ask selected groups to share some ideas for one of the situations with the class.

12 Good business

LANGUAGE SUMMARY

Topics/Functions: A small business/coffee shop; discussing what makes a business successful
Structures: Infinitive clauses and phrases of purpose

STORY SUMMARY

Jacob interviews Lili Chen, the owner of a successful café located near the university he attends, for Campus TV. They talk about the factors that make a café successful.

Preview

CULTURE

The culture note introduces the topic of cafés (also known as coffee shops or coffeehouses) and gives some background information about cafés in the U.S. in order to build interest in and increase overall understanding of the video.

• Have students read the culture note silently. Then answer their questions about vocabulary or content.
• Read the questions aloud, and have students work in small groups to answer them.
• Check answers around the class.

VOCABULARY

In this activity, students practice using vocabulary to talk about cafés by completing a cloze passage and then quizzing a partner with definitions of the words.

A
• Explain the task, and lead students through the passage, the example, and the words in the box.
• Have students work in pairs to complete the task. Have pairs join together to compare answers in small groups.
• Check answers as a class.

Answers
A: I'm looking for a place to get a **great** cup of coffee.
B: How about Gino's Grind? It's nearby, so it's very **convenient**.
A: Do they have **comfortable** chairs?
B: Yes, they do. Gino's is small and **cozy**. It's **popular** with all the students.
A: I want to be able to have a conversation without shouting. Is the music very **loud**?
B: No, it's not. And they have nice things to eat there, too. The owner makes **fresh** pastries every morning.
A: That's good, but you know the real secret to a **successful** coffee shop is delicious coffee.
B: You said it! And Gino's coffee is fantastic. Let's go!

B
• Explain the task, and go over the example language.
• Have students work in pairs to complete the task.

3 GUESS THE FACTS

In this activity, students prepare to watch the video by using visual information to make predictions about the people in the video.

• Explain the task, and direct students' attention to the photos.
• Have students work alone to make their predictions. Then have students compare predictions with a partner. Encourage them to give reasons for their guesses.

- Ask selected students to share their predictions with the class. Don't tell students the answers yet. Tell students they will find out if their predictions are correct in the next activity.

Answers

1. café owner   2. reporter

 Watch the video

4 GET THE PICTURE

In these activities, students watch and listen to the video to find out what the café owner says are the reasons for her success. They then match a description with the correct picture.

A

- Explain the task, and lead students through the statements.
- Play the entire video with the sound on. Have students work alone to complete the task as they watch. Have students compare answers with a partner.
- Check answers around the class.

Answers

Students like to do their homework at the café.
The music is always good.
There are comfortable chairs.
The café is close to campus.

B

- Explain the task. Direct students' attention to the pictures and lead them through the statements.
- Have students work alone to complete the task. Ask students if they need to watch the video again and replay if necessary.
- Have students compare answers with a partner, and then check answers around the class.

Answers

(from left to right)
3, 1, 4, 2

5 WATCH FOR DETAILS

In this activity, students focus on details in the video in order to complete statements about the video.

- Explain the task, and read through the list of statements.
- Have students work alone to predict the answers to as many questions as they can before they watch the video again.
- Play the entire video with the sound on. Have students work alone to check their predictions and complete the task.
- Have students compare answers with a partner. Then check answers as a class.

Answers

1. owner	5. outside/on
2. location	campus
3. it didn't have	6. stay a long time
comfortable chairs	7. music
4. a pastry	8. students

6 WHAT'S YOUR OPINION?

In these activities, students personalize the topic of the unit by asking classmates for their opinions about cafés.

A

- Explain the task, and lead students through the chart.
- Have students work alone to add their own question to the chart. Then have them work in groups to complete the task. Make sure students understand they should answer according to their own opinion and give reasons for their answers.

B

- Explain the task. Ask selected groups to share their answers to one of the questions and give reasons.

 **Follow-up**

 7 OPEN YOUR OWN CAFÉ

In this communicative activity, students have the chance to be creative by imagining they are going to open a café and deciding what their café will be like.

A

- Explain the task, and lead students through the questions.
- Have students work in pairs to answer the questions and plan their new café.

B

- Explain the task, and have pairs join together with another pair to complete the task.
- Ask selected pairs to share what their café will be like with the class.

 Language close-up

 8 WHAT DID THEY SAY?

This cloze activity develops bottom-up listening skills by having students focus on specific language from the video.

- Explain the task. Have students work alone or in pairs to read the text and fill in as many blanks as they can before watching the video.
- Play this segment of the video with the sound on while students work alone to fill in the blanks and check their predictions. Then have students compare answers with a partner.
- Check answers as a class.
- If time permits, ask for volunteers to stand up and act out the conversation.

> **Answers**
>
> Jacob: What **about** the food?
> Lili: Our food is made here **fresh** every morning. We have a **strong** take-out business. People order food to take home or to eat **outside**.
> Jacob: **Outside**? You mean, on the **grass**, on campus?

> Lili: **Anywhere**. We do have tables outside, too. But **people** do eat on campus. It's really **pretty** there.
> Jacob: But it's nice to sit **inside**, too. The atmosphere is great **here**. Talk about that for a minute: the **lights**, the **music**.
> Lili: Music is key to a café's **success**. You need to **make sure** you have good music. I'm not an **expert**. I mean, I don't know **much** about music. But people who work here are **students**. They're **tuned in**. They know what's **popular**. So I let them **choose** the music.

9 INFINITIVE CLAUSES AND PHRASES OF PURPOSE

In these activities, students practice the functional and grammatical focus of the unit by using infinitive clauses and phrases of purpose to complete sentences about factors that make a business successful.

A

- Explain the task, and read the example aloud.
- Have students work alone to complete the task. Put students into pairs to compare answers.
- Check answers as a class, and review the structure as necessary.

> **Answers**
> 1. In order to
> 2. In order for
> 3. In order for
> 4. In order to

B

- Explain the task, and read the example aloud.
- Have students work alone to complete the task. Put students into pairs to compare answers.
- Check answers as a class, and review the structure as necessary.

> **Answers**
> 1. because
> 2. The reason
> 3. because of
> 4. for

13 Stonehenge

LANGUAGE SUMMARY

Topics/Functions: *Stonehenge; explaining past events*
Structures: *Past modals for degrees of certainty*

STORY SUMMARY

This documentary is about Stonehenge, an ancient site in Wiltshire, U.K. The video presents some facts about Stonehenge and speculations about how and why it was built, as well as what it might have been used for.

Preview

1 CULTURE

The culture note presents interesting information about ancient stone circles similar to Stonehenge in order to build interest in and increase overall understanding of the video.

- Have students read the culture note silently. Then answer their questions about vocabulary or content.
- Read the questions aloud, and have students work in small groups to answer them.
- Check answers around the class.

2 VOCABULARY

In this activity, students work with key vocabulary related to Stonehenge, including terms used in the video.

- Explain the task. Read through the sentences and answer choices, and go over the example.
- Have students work individually or in pairs to complete the task. Then put students in pairs or groups of four to compare answers.
- Check answers as a class.

Answers

1. huge
2. holy place
3. basic
4. used for special rituals
5. burned bodies
6. uncover by digging out earth

3 GUESS THE FACTS

In this activity, students prepare to watch the video by using visual information to make predictions about the story.

- Explain the task, and lead students through the list of experts.
- Play the first minute of the video with the sound off (until the sunset view of Stonehenge). Tell students to look for the answers as they watch.
- Have students work alone to check off their answers. Then have students compare answers with a partner.
- Check predictions around the class, but don't tell students the answers yet. Tell students they will find out if their predictions are correct in the next activity.

Watch the video

4 GET THE PICTURE

In these activities, students watch and listen to match facts from the video to the correct pictures.

A

- Explain the task, and read the facts aloud.
- Play the entire video with the sound on. Have students work alone to complete the task. Have them compare answers with a partner before checking answers as a class.

Answers

(from left to right)
a   d   b   c

B

- Explain the task, and read the words and phrases aloud.
- Ask students if they want to watch the video again. Have students work alone to complete the task. Then have them compare answers with a partner.
- Check answers as a class.

Answers

(from left to right)
a monumental undertaking
a place to commune with the spirits
an excavation
a part of the ceremonial complex

5 WATCH FOR DETAILS

In this activity, students focus more closely on details in the video in order to determine whether statements about the content of the documentary are true or false.

- Explain the task, and read the statements in the chart.

- Have students work alone to predict the answers to as many of the questions as they can.
- Play the entire video with the sound on. Have students work alone to check their predictions and check off their answers as they watch.
- Have students compare answers with a partner.
- Check answers as a class.

Answers

1. False (Stonehenge/It is located in England.)
2. False (Stonehenge/It contains about 153 stones.)
3. True
4. False (Nobody knows who built Stonehenge/it.)
5. True
6. True
7. False (Blue Stonehenge/It was discovered in 2009. Cremated remains were discovered in 2008.)
8. True

6 WHAT'S YOUR OPINION?

In these activities, students give their opinions about the likelihood of the origins of Stonehenge presented in the video by ranking them. Then they compare opinions with a partner.

A

- Explain the task, and lead students through the statements. Make sure students understand they should answer according to their own opinion.
- Have students work alone to complete the task.

B

- Explain the task. Put students into pairs to complete the task.
- Ask selected pairs to share their opinions of one of the explanations with the class.

Follow-up

7 WHAT DO YOU THINK HAPPENED?

In this activity, students have the opportunity to discuss stories about two other unexplained phenomena – the Tunguska event in Russia and the disappearance of the Maya in parts of Central America and present-day Mexico – and what might have happened in these cases.

A

- Explain the task, and have students read the two passages silently. Answer any questions about vocabulary or content.

B

- Call attention to the model dialog, and practice it with two volunteers.
- Have students work in groups of three to talk about what might have happened. Encourage students to give reasons for their opinions.
- If time permits, ask select groups to share their ideas with the class.

Language close-up

8 WHAT DID THEY SAY?

This cloze activity develops bottom-up listening skills by having students focus on specific language from the video.

- Explain the task. Have students work alone or in pairs to read the text and fill in as many blanks as they can before watching the video.
- Play this segment of the video with the sound on while students work alone to fill in the blanks and check their predictions. Then have students compare answers with a partner.
- Check answers as a class.

Answers

Richards: The **period** we're **dealing** with here is our **prehistory**, and what **defines** prehistory is that we've got no **written records** about **anything**. So

everything that we understand about it comes from archaeology, from **what** we can excavate and what we can **analyze**.

Narrator: In 2008, **hundreds** of **human** bones were **excavated** at the **site**, primitively burned and **buried**. The bones were dated across a **thousand** years of prehistory.

Richards: The first **analysis** of all the cremated **bones** that were **found** at Stonehenge **suggests** that it's **mainly** adult **males**, adult men that were **buried** there. So it's quite a **distinctive** group of people, and only probably very **important** people came **there** to be buried.

9 PASSIVE AND PAST MODALS

In this activity, students practice the grammatical and functional focus of the unit by using past modals to express an opinion.

- Explain the task, and go over the example.
- Have students work alone to complete the task. Then put students into pairs to compare answers.
- Check answers as a class.

Answers

1. Stone circles must have been used by ancient peoples for rituals.
2. The Mayan people might have been saved by better farming practices.
3. The Mayans could have been killed by an infectious disease.
4. Eighty million trees in Tunguska may have been destroyed by a small comet.
5. Vehicles with wheels couldn't have been used by the builders of Stonehenge.
6. Archaeologists must have been surprised by the discovery of a second circle at Stonehenge.

14 Making music

LANGUAGE SUMMARY

Topics/Functions: *Creating music; describing the steps in a process*
Structures: *The passive to describe process*

STORY SUMMARY

This documentary shows how music is made – from the creative process to a finished song that's played on the radio. First, a singer/songwriter talks about how he writes and records a song. Next, a recording engineer talks about his role in recording music. Finally, various people at a radio station talk about what they do in addition to broadcasting music.

 **Preview**

1 CULTURE

The culture note introduces the topic of music by presenting information about how music is accessed today in order to build interest in the topic and increase overall understanding of the video.

- Have students read the culture note silently. Then answer their questions about vocabulary or content.
- Read the questions aloud, and have students work in small groups to answer them.
- Check answers around the class.

2 VOCABULARY

In this activity, students work with vocabulary from the video by completing sentences that describe making music.

A

- Explain the task. Lead students through the words in the box and the sentences. Go over the example.
- Have students work alone to complete the task. Have students compare answers with a partner before checking them as a class.

Answers
1. compose
2. set up
3. tune
4. accompany
5. record
6. mix

B

- Explain the task.
- Have students work in pairs to complete the task.
- Ask selected students to share one of their original sentences with the class.

3 GUESS THE FACTS

In this activity, students prepare to watch the video by predicting the job duties of four people who work in the music business.

- Explain the task, and lead students through the job titles.
- Have students work alone to make their predictions. Have students compare their predictions with a partner.
- Ask a few students to share their predictions with the class. Don't tell students the answers yet. Tell them they will find out if their predictions are correct in Exercise 5.

Watch the video

4 GET THE PICTURE

In this activity, students watch and listen to match the people in the video with their job titles.

- Explain the task, and read the names and job titles.
- Play the entire video with the sound on. Have students work alone to complete the task as they watch.
- Put students into pairs to compare answers before checking them as a class.

Answers

Josh McBride: DJ
Richard Marr: recording engineer
Aldous Collins: accompanist
Melanie Oliver: program director
Matthew Hawkes: songwriter

5 WATCH FOR DETAILS

In this activity, students focus more closely on details in order to match the job titles in Exercise 4 to their descriptions.

A

- Explain the task, and read through the sentences. Make sure students understand that they should use the job titles from Exercise 4 to complete the sentences.
- Play the entire video with the sound on. Have students work alone to complete the task as they watch.
- Have students compare answers with a partner before checking answers as a class.

Answers

1. recording engineer
2. DJ
3. accompanist
4. songwriter
5. program director

B

- Explain the task, and read the example aloud.
- Have students work in pairs to complete the task. Have pairs join together with another pair to compare answers.
- Ask selected pairs to share details about the jobs with the class.

 # Follow-up

6 WRITING A SONG

In these activities, students have a chance to be creative by imagining they are songwriters and planning how they will record and promote their new song.

A

- Explain the task, and lead students through the questions.
- Have students work individually to complete the task.

B

- Explain the task, and read the instructions aloud.
- Have students work in pairs to complete the task.
- Ask selected pairs to share their plans with the class.

7 WHICH JOB WOULD YOU LIKE?

In this activity, students personalize the topic of the video by discussing which job in the music industry appeals to them.

A

- Explain the task, and read the instructions aloud.
- Put students into pairs to complete the task. Encourage students to give reasons for their choices.

B

- Explain the task, and read the instructions aloud.
- Have pairs join together with another pair to complete the task.
- Ask selected students to share their job preference with the class.

 Language close-up

8 WHAT DID THEY SAY?

This cloze activity develops bottom-up listening skills by having students focus on specific language from the video.

- Explain the task. Have students work alone or in pairs to read the text and fill in as many blanks as they can before watching the video.
- Play this segment of the video with the sound on while students work alone to fill in the blanks and check their predictions. Then have students compare answers with a partner.
- Check answers as a class.

> **Answers**
>
> Matthew: Making music is my **creative** outlet: the way I make **sense** of the world **around** me. **When** I sit down to **compose**, the first thing I do is **tune** my guitar. Once the **guitar** is tuned up and **ready**, I set up the keyboard. The **keyboard** has multiple **functions** and multiple **sounds**. What comes **out** of **me** is a **reflection** of **how** I'm **feeling** that **day**. Sometimes I can **spend** hours writing **one** piece. I'm **writing** this song. I **titled** it "Revelations."
>
>   *   *   *
>
> Melanie: Hi, my name's Melanie Oliver. I'm the **program director** here at the **radio station**. The program director's job is to **decide** what music is **played** on air. So I **pick** the songs and tell the DJs **what** songs to play.

9 PASSIVE

In these activities, students practice the grammatical and functional focus of the unit by using the passive to complete sentences about a process. They then number the steps in order to explain the process.

A

- Explain the task, and lead students through the incomplete sentences.
- Have students work alone to complete the task. Then put students into pairs to compare answers.
- Check answers as a class.

> **Answers**
>
> is recorded
> is played
> is taken, is added
> is composed
> is chosen
> are mixed

B

- Explain the task, and go over the example.
- Put students into pairs to complete the task. Have pairs get together with another pair to compare answers before checking them with the class.

> **Answers**
>
> 2 The song is recorded on a multitrack recorder.
> 6 The song is played on the radio by the DJ.
> 4 The recording is taken to program directors at radio stations and is added to their playlists.
> 1 The song is composed by the songwriter.
> 5 The song is chosen for airplay by the program director.
> 3 The vocals and instruments are mixed together.

15 The streets of Montreal

LANGUAGE SUMMARY

Topics/Functions: Controversy in a city; expressing opinions about city rules
        Structures: Passive modals

STORY SUMMARY

In this documentary, Kai Nagata interviews people about bike lanes and cycling in Montreal, Quebec, Canada. He asks people for their opinions about the bike lanes in Montreal, bike safety rules including wearing helmets, and how they think cycling safety can be improved.

 **Preview**

1 CULTURE

The culture note introduces the topic of the video by presenting some interesting information about the increase in cycling as a means of transportation in the U.S. and Canada.

- Have students read the culture note silently. Then answer their questions about vocabulary or content.
- Read the questions aloud, and have students work in small groups to answer them.
- Check answers around the class.

2 VOCABULARY

In this activity, students work with key vocabulary related to cycling and city traffic by completing sentences with words from the video.

- Explain the task, and lead students through the words in the box, the sentences, and the example.
- Have students work alone to complete the task. Then put students into pairs to compare their answers.
- Check answers as a class.

> **Answers**
> 1. sidewalk
> 2. commuters

> 3. Cyclists
> 4. Pedestrians
> 5. traffic
> 6. drivers
> 7. Buses
> 8. bike helmet
> 9. cycle path
> 10. parking

3 GUESS THE FACTS

In this activity, students prepare to watch the video by using visual information to make predictions about the story.

- Explain the task, and read the questions aloud.
- Play the first minute of the video with the sound off (until the close-up on the black car), and tell students to watch for the answers.
- Have selected students share one of their predictions with the class. Don't tell students the answers yet. Tell them they will find out if their predictions are correct in the next activity.

> **Answers**
> 1. He's a TV reporter.
> 2. He's in Montreal, Quebec, Canada.
> 3. He's talking to people about cycling in the city.

Watch the video

4 GET THE PICTURE

In this activity, students watch and listen to the video in order to determine what issues the people talk about in the video.

- Explain the task. Tell students to look at the photos and read the statements below each one.
- Play the entire video with the sound on. Have students work alone to complete the task. Have students compare their answers with a partner.
- Check answers as a class.

Answers

1. Cycle paths
2. Driving toward traffic
3. Restricting driving downtown
4. Cycling with children
5. Bicycles and buses
6. Riding with headphones
7. Cycling with children

5 WHO SAID WHAT?

In this activity, students watch and listen more closely to determine who said certain things in the video.

- Explain the task, and lead students through the list of statements and the example.
- Have students work alone to predict any answers they can before watching the video again.
- Play the entire video with the sound on. Have students work alone to check their predictions and correct answers as necessary.
- Have students compare their answers with a partner before checking them as a class.

Answers

5 "I think it would be best if bicycles and buses were not on the same street."

2 "Cyclists should have their own bike lane and drive towards the oncoming traffic."

7 "I think cycling on the sidewalk is fine, with kids."

4 "There should be a law that says all children starting from age six should be educated on the rules of bicycling."

1 "I think the city should try to expand the system of cycle paths."

3 "Maybe some restrictions to driving downtown . . . "

6 "I'd like to bike and listen to music too, but . . . I think you should do that in a park."

6 GUESSING MEANING FROM CONTEXT

In this activity, students use context clues to figure out the meaning of words used in the video.

- Explain the task, and read the statements and answer choices aloud. Remind students to use clues in other parts of the sentence to figure out the meaning of the underlined words.
- Have students work alone to complete the task and then compare answers with a partner.
- Check answers as a class.

Answers

1. allowing others space on the road
2. relate to each other
3. comfortable
4. pay attention to
5. try to save time
6. is the same as other places

Follow-up

7 FOR OR AGAINST

In these activities, students practice giving opinions for and against bike lanes.

A

- Explain the task, and direct students' attention to the chart.
- Have students work alone to complete the task.

B

- Explain the task, and read the example language.

- Have students work in groups of four to complete the task. Tell students they must reach a decision at the end of their discussion.
- Have a volunteer from each group share their decision with the class. Ask them to include their reasons for the decision.

Language close-up

8 WHAT DID THEY SAY?

This cloze activity develops bottom-up listening skills by having students focus on specific language from the video.

- Explain the task. Have students work alone or in pairs to read the text and fill in as many blanks as they can before watching the video.
- Play this segment of the video with the sound on while students work alone to fill in the blanks and check their predictions. Then have students compare answers with a partner.
- Check answers as a class.
- If time permits, ask for volunteers to stand up and read the text aloud.

Answers

Sebastian: I think the city should try to **expand** the system of **cycle** paths. One thing I **learned** this morning is that one **shouldn't** drive **against** traffic because that's a **problem**. Sometimes there are corners where **drivers** just cannot see you coming, and so you should really try to **avoid** driving against the **traffic**, if possible.

* * *

Nitai: Cyclists should have their own bike **lane** and drive towards the **oncoming** traffic **because** they will be able to better see **what** the other **parked** cars are doing, **whether** they're driving or **parked**, the cyclist will have more **control**.

9 PASSIVE MODALS

In this activity, students practice the grammatical and functional focus of the unit by using passive modals to talk about city rules.

- Explain the task, and read through the complaints from cyclists and motorists. Point out the modals and the example.
- Have students work alone to complete the task. Have students compare answers with a partner.
- Discuss answers as a class.

Possible answers
1. Drivers shouldn't be permitted to go faster than the speed limit.
2. Drivers shouldn't be allowed to park in bike lanes.
3. Drivers ought to be required to check their rearview mirrors before opening their doors.
4. Cyclists must be required to put lights on their bikes when riding at night.
5. Cyclists have to be required to wear bike helmets.
6. Cyclists shouldn't be permitted to ignore traffic signals.

16 The Harlem Children's Zone

LANGUAGE SUMMARY

Topics/Functions: *Education; talking about challenges*

Structures: *Complex noun phrases with gerunds*

STORY SUMMARY

In this news report, Anderson Cooper interviews Geoffrey Canada, who has an ambitious plan for improving education for underprivileged children in the U.S. The report focuses on a school in New York City called the Promise Academy that is part of a larger project called the Harlem Children's Zone.

Note: This is an excerpt from a longer piece. The entire segment is included on the DVD as a bonus track for teachers who want to use it for extended viewing practice.

 **Preview**

 CULTURE

The culture note presents some background information about educational challenges in underprivileged neighborhoods in the U.S. in order to increase understanding of the video.

- Have students read the culture note silently. Then answer their questions about vocabulary or content.
- Read the questions aloud, and have students work in small groups to answer them.
- Check answers around the class.

2 VOCABULARY

In this activity, students work with vocabulary to talk about education in a broad context.

A

- Explain the task. Lead students through the phrases in the box, the sentences, and the example.
- Have students work alone to complete the task.

B

- Explain the task. Put students in pairs to complete the task.
- Have pairs compare their answers with another pair.
- Check answers as a class.

Answers
1. break the cycle
2. inner city
3. affluent suburbs
4. achievement gap
5. grade level
6. scientific data
7. remarkable job
8. statistical study

3 GUESS THE FACTS

In this activity, students prepare to watch the video by using visual information to make predictions about what happens in the video.

- Explain the task, and read the questions aloud.
- Play the first minute and a half of the video with the sound off (until we see the reporter listening, hands folded), and tell students to watch for the answers.

- Check predictions as a class, but don't tell students the answers yet. Tell students they will find out if their predictions are correct in the next activity.

> **Answers**
> 1. They're an educator (Geoffrey Canada) and a reporter (Anderson Cooper).
> 2. They're talking about education for children in the inner city.
> 3. They take place in a school in the inner city (run by Geoffrey Canada).

Watch the video

 ## 4 GET THE PICTURE

In this activity, students watch and listen in order to answer some general questions about the school featured in the video.

- Explain the task, and lead students through the statements.
- Play the entire video with the sound on, and have students work alone to complete the task as they watch.
- Have students compare their answers with a partner, and replay the video if necessary.
- Check answers as a class.

> **Answers**
> It is a school for kids from the inner city.
> It is a charter school run by Geoffrey Canada.
> Students are in class more often than in other schools.
> It improves learning skills and test scores for its students.

5 WATCH FOR DETAILS

In these activities, students watch and listen more closely to determine if statements about the school are true or false. Then they correct the false statements and talk about other details they learned with a partner.

A

- Explain the task, and read through the statements in the chart. Review the example and answer any vocabulary questions as they arise.
- Have students work alone to answer as many questions as they can before watching the video.
- Play the entire video with the sound on. Tell students to complete the task as they watch.
- Have students work alone to check their predictions and correct answers as necessary. Have students compare their answers with a partner.
- Check answers as a class.

> **Answers**
> 1. True
> 2. False (He wants all of his students to go to college.)
> 3. False (He grew up in the South Bronx.)
> 4. False (There is one adult for every six children.)
> 5. True
> 6. True
> 7. True
> 8. False (He will know it has worked when he sees his kids by the thousands with degrees./ He will know it has worked when people look for kids from Harlem.)

B

- Explain the task.
- Have students work in pairs to complete the task.
- If time permits, ask selected students to share some additional details they remember with the class.

6 GUESSING MEANING FROM CONTEXT

In this activity, students use context clues to figure out the meanings of words used in the video.

- Explain the task, and read the statements and answer choices aloud.

- Have students work alone to complete the task. Then put students into pairs to compare answers.
- Check answers as a class.

> **Answers**
> 1. difference
> 2. left forever
> 3. variety
> 4. amazing
> 5. in the future

 Follow-up

7 WHAT'S YOUR OPINION?

In these activities, students personalize the information in the video by ranking different qualities that are important in a successful school.

A
- Explain the task, and lead students through the list. Make sure students understand they should answer according to their own opinion.
- Have students work alone to complete the task.

B
- Explain the task, and model the sample dialog.
- Have students work in pairs to complete the task. Encourage students to give reasons for their rankings.
- Have pairs join together with another pair to compare answers. Ask volunteers to share their ideas with the class.

 **Language close-up**

8 WHAT DID THEY SAY?

This cloze activity develops bottom-up listening skills by having students focus on specific language from the video.

- Explain the task. Have students work alone or in pairs to read the text and fill in as many blanks as they can before watching the video.
- Play this segment of the video with the sound on while students work alone to fill in the blanks and check their predictions. Then have students compare answers with a partner.
- Check answers as a class.

> **Answers**
> Reporter: What is the **racial** achievement gap?
> Dr. Fryer: Black **children** in our schools are not **performing** at even **close** the rate as white children in our schools. The **average** black seventeen-year-old **reads** at the proficiency **level** of the **average** white thirteen-year-old. A four-year **difference** in effective **reading skills**: that's . . . that's **huge**.
> Reporter: But when Dr. Fryer **analyzed** four years' worth of Promise Academy **test** scores, he **discovered** something **remarkable**.
> Dr. Fryer: At the **elementary** school level, he **closed** the achievement **gap** in **both** subjects: **math** and reading.
> Reporter: **Actually** eliminating the **gap** in elementary **school**?
> Dr. Fryer: Absolutely. We've **never** seen . . . we've **never** seen anything **like** that.

9 COMPLEX NOUN PHRASES WITH GERUNDS

In these activities, students practice both the grammatical and functional focus of the unit by using complex noun phrases with gerunds to interview a partner about meeting a challenge.

A
- Explain the task, and read through the questions with the class. Review the example.

- Have students work in pairs to complete the task. Make sure students tell something about their challenge before their partner chooses which questions to ask.

> **Possible answers**
>
> (*Note:* Answers will depend on which questions were asked and how the partner answered, but should start like below.)
> 1. The most challenging part was . . .
> 2. One of the rewards was . . .
> 3. The most dangerous part was . . .
> 4. The easiest part was . . .
> 5. The most surprising thing was . . .
> 6. The most exciting thing was . . .
> 7. The scariest thing was . . .
> 8. The funniest thing was . . .

B

- Explain the task.
- Have pairs get together with another pair to take turns telling about their partner's challenging experience.
- If time permits, ask volunteers to share their partner's challenging experience with the class.

Video Transcripts

Unit 1: Dream Date

A young woman chooses one of three men for her date on a dating game show.

Host: Hello, everyone, and welcome to *Dream Date*, the show where one lucky lady gets to choose her perfect date. I'm your host, Richard Darien. Now, let's meet our contestant: She's an English teacher from Chicago, Illinois. She's 25 years old, interested in American history, literature, and the arts. Ladies and gentlemen, meet Elizabeth Campbell. . . . *(to Elizabeth)* Hello, Elizabeth, and welcome to *Dream Date*.

Elizabeth: Hi, Richard. I'm delighted to be here.

Host: So tell us, Elizabeth, what qualities do you look for in a guy?

Elizabeth: I like a guy who is honest and straightforward, someone who is considerate and interested in other people.

Host: Is there anything you don't like in a guy?

Elizabeth: Yes. I don't like when a guy is egotistical – when he talks about himself all the time. That is something that really bothers me.

Host: I know what you mean. Well, it's time to meet our bachelors. Bachelor Number 1 is a writer and a former college soccer star who loves watching almost any kind of sport. Bachelor Number 2 is the Director of Educational Programs at a science museum, and in his free time, he enjoys reading, running, and camping. Bachelor Number 3 is a model, who also studies marketing. He says everyone should recognize him from his latest running shoe ad on billboards and in magazines. Welcome, gentlemen. It's good to have you with us. OK, let's get started. . . . *(to Elizabeth)* What is your first question?

Elizabeth: Bachelor Number 1. If you were with your friends and were late to our first date, what excuse would you give?

Bachelor 1: Well, I'd be too embarrassed to tell you the truth, so I'd probably say I had car trouble or got stuck in traffic or something.

Elizabeth: OK. Bachelor Number 2, same question.

Bachelor 2: Well, it bothers me when people lie, so I would tell you the truth and hope you were generous enough to forgive me.

Elizabeth: Bachelor Number 3?

Bachelor 3: Well, I'd probably tell you what I tell everyone else: "It's hard to split my time among so many people!"

Elizabeth: OK. Next question. Bachelor Number 1, describe to me your ideal date.

Bachelor 1: Getting together with a bunch of my friends, having a barbecue, and watching sports on TV. Yeah, that'd be a great date.

Elizabeth: OK. Bachelor Number 2?

Bachelor 2: I'd take you out for a nice dinner. Let's just relax and enjoy the evening and get to know each other.

Elizabeth: Bachelor Number 2, tell me two things about yourself: one positive and one negative.

Bachelor 2: Well, I think I'm a pretty good friend; very reliable. Something negative? I'm very direct, and that sometimes upsets people.

Elizabeth: No, I think that's a good thing. Bachelor Number 3: something good and something not so good about yourself.

Bachelor 3: Well, I'm actually a pretty good guy. As for something not so good: I can't think of anything.

Host: OK, Elizabeth. Final question, and then you're going to have to make your choice.

Elizabeth: Right. Bachelor Number 1, finish this sentence: "I can't stand it when . . ."

Bachelor 1: I can't stand it when . . . people talk when I'm trying to watch the soccer match on TV.

Elizabeth: Bachelor Number 3, finish this sentence: "I think it's disgusting when . . ."

Bachelor 3: I think it's disgusting when . . . when I go to a fancy restaurant and I don't get the service I deserve.

Elizabeth: Bachelor Number 2, finish this sentence: "It really bothers me when . . ."

Bachelor 2: It really bothers me when . . . people argue over unimportant things. I just think people should be less temperamental and more relaxed.

Host: We are out of time. Now, I'm going to ask you to make a choice.

Elizabeth: I think I'm going to choose Bachelor Number 2.

Host: Are you sure?

Elizabeth: Yes.

Host: All right. Well, let's meet this guy! Bachelor Number 2 comes from Chicago, your own hometown! Elizabeth, meet Adam York!

Elizabeth: Adam York?

Adam: Betty? Betty Campbell?

Elizabeth: Adam!

Adam: I knew it!

Host: Wait a minute. You two know each other?

Elizabeth: We went to high school together!

Host: Well, that takes the mystery out of the show. I'm your host, Richard Darien. Thanks for joining us. See you next time on *Dream Date*!

Unit 2: Career moves

A career advisor talks about the importance of someone's personality type in choosing a major and profession.

Jamie: Welcome to Matheson College. I'm Jamie Fitch. Some students arrive on campus with clear career ambitions, but most students need some help figuring out which field of study is right for them. The good news is, help is available. I'm here with Jacquelyn Auden, a career advisor from the Career Services Department here on campus. . . . (*to Ms. Auden*) Ms. Auden, you've advised a lot of students over the years about choosing a major and a career path. What should students consider?

Ms. Auden: Well, Jamie, one of the first things to consider is your personality type. Along with your skills, abilities, and personal preferences, your personality type can guide you toward finding a major that best suits you.

Jamie: OK, so how many personality types are there?

Ms. Auden: There are six basic personality types: artistic, conventional, enterprising, investigative, realistic, and social. The first type is artistic: These people are creative and imaginative, and they prefer to work on one project at a time, rather than multi-tasking.

Jamie: What careers should artistic types pursue?

Ms. Auden: The most important thing for this type of people is being in charge of a creative project. So, careers to consider are landscaping, graphic design, web design.

Jamie: I see. The next personality type is conventional. Tell us about that one.

Ms. Auden: Yes. Conventional types are practical and orderly. They respond well to rules, procedures, schedules, things like that.

Jamie: What types of careers do conventional-type people usually enjoy?

Ms. Auden: Conventional types often enjoy numbers, and they're also good with measuring and analyzing things in general. So often they tend to be bankers, lawyers, building inspectors, and technical writers.

Jamie: Are they good businesspeople?

Ms. Auden: Sure, they can be, but they usually work for others. The next type, enterprising people, those are the business owners.

Jamie: Ah, the enterprising type. What characteristics do those people share?

Ms. Auden: They tend to be leaders. They're independent and willing to take risks. They're good at motivating people, so we often find them in sales.

Jamie: Really! What careers do they enjoy, aside from sales?

Ms. Auden: Well, they're good at directing projects and people, so they make good managers.

Jamie: OK, so that's three types. Let's take a look at the fourth type: investigative.

Ms. Auden: This type of person prefers logic to imagination and tends to be precise and detailed. So, Jamie, what are some careers that you think would suit this type of person?

Jamie: Hmm. Science would probably be appealing.

Ms. Auden: You're right. Uncovering mysteries is key to any type of science. But librarians are also the investigative type. Really, any career that involves research fits into this category.

Jamie: So that brings us up to the fifth type: realistic.

Ms. Auden: Yes. Realistic types like to work with their hands, with tools. They want to see the results of their work in physical terms.

Jamie: That sounds like repair people to me.

Ms. Auden: Yes, that's right. Also jewelry makers, builders, and engineers.

Jamie: So, now for the sixth personality type, which is the one that describes me best.

Ms. Auden: Yes, I think you're right. The last type is social. Social types like people. Their jobs usually involve helping and communicating with others.

Jamie: I'll bet teaching would appeal to social types.

Ms. Auden: Oh, yes. Medicine, coaching, broadcast journalism, and of course, career advising.

Jamie: That's us, social types. . . . (*to Ms. Auden*) Ms. Auden, thank you for sharing this information with us.

Ms. Auden: It was my pleasure, Jamie.

Jamie: (*to camera*) Well, we hope this information has been helpful to you. If you'd like to learn more, visit the Career Services Department, and tell them Jamie sent you.

     Interchange 3 Video transcripts © Cambridge University Press 2012   *Photocopiable*

Six Personality Types

	Characteristics	**Careers**
Artistic	creative & imaginative focus on single projects	landscaping graphic design web design
Conventional	practical & orderly respond well to rules	banking law building inspection technical writing
Enterprising	independent & risk-taking motivate others	business / sales management
Investigative	logical & precise tend to focus on details	science library science research
Realistic	hands-on & physical work well with tools	repair jewelry making construction engineering
Social	prefer to work with others helpful & communicative	teaching medicine coaching broadcast journalism career advising

Unit 3: Common ground

A woman asks her friend to look after her younger sister overnight.

Anne: Rachel! I am so glad you're home. I was wondering if you could help me out.

Rachel: Yeah. What's up, Anne?

Anne: I need a big favor. My boss just called, and he wants me to go out of town this afternoon to meet with a client.

Rachel: That's great.

Anne: Yeah. But my parents are out of town, too, and my little sister, Megan, is staying with me. Would you mind if she stayed with you tonight? I could pick her up tomorrow by ten.

Rachel: No, I don't mind at all. What time did you want to bring her over?

Anne: How about now?

Rachel: Hi, Megan. Did you want to spend the night here?

Megan: OK.

Rachel: Great. But I have a report to work on tonight. . . .

Anne: Don't worry. We planned ahead. She brought her homework. She'll keep herself busy.

Rachel: Fantastic.

Anne: I have to run. Thanks a million.

Rachel: Oh, you're welcome.

Anne: Bye, Meg! Have fun, but do your homework, OK?

Megan: Don't worry, Anne. I will.

Rachel: Bye.

*   *   *

Rachel: What grade are you in, Megan?

Megan: Eighth. Hey, you've got the *Twilight* movies! Can we watch them?

Rachel: Sure. But I think you should do your homework first.

Megan: OK.

Rachel: Good. You can work in here. I have some work to do, too, so I'm going to go to my office.

Megan: OK.

*   *   *

Rachel: Hey, kiddo. How's the homework coming?

Megan: Good. I did half of my math problems.

Rachel: That's good, but you still have some more work to do. You can watch the movie when you're done, OK?

*   *   *

Megan: Rachel!?

Rachel: Yes?

Megan: I'm done! Is it OK if I watch the movie now?

Rachel: Yes!

*   *   *

Rachel: Megan, could you turn that down a little bit?

Megan: What?

Rachel: Could you please turn down the volume?

Megan: Oh.

Rachel: Thank you.

Megan: I'm starving. Could I have something to eat?

Rachel: It's only four in the afternoon.

Megan: So?

Rachel: Um, OK. How about some carrot sticks and an apple?

Megan: What else have you got?

Rachel: I have some strawberries and whipped cream.

Megan: Anything else?

Rachel: OK. How about a pizza? I have one in the freezer.

Megan: Plain?

Rachel: I think it's a veggie pizza.

Megan: That sounds good.

Rachel: OK.

*   *   *

Rachel: I love this part.

Megan: I know. It's so romantic when Edward tells her he loves her. Does he stay with her?

Rachel: You mean you've never read any of the books or seen the movies?

Megan: No, I was too little. But I'm old enough to understand them now! Can we watch the second movie after this one's over?

Rachel: I have a better idea.

*   *   *

Anne: Hello? Anybody home?

Rachel: Good morning.

Megan: Good morning.

Anne: Good morning. What's going on here?

Megan: We stayed up late reading *Twilight*. . . . (*to Rachel*) I loved it when Bella first dreamed about Edward.

Rachel: Oh, me, too. The part where Jacob appears. Wow. . . . (*to Anne*) We must have lost track of time.

Anne: We ought to get going, Megan.

Megan: All right, I'll grab my stuff. . . . (*to Rachel*) These books are the best. Would you mind if I borrowed this one?

Rachel: Oh, no, go ahead.

Megan: Thanks!

Anne: You two really seemed to hit it off. How'd you do it?

Rachel: I guess a good book can still bring people together.

Unit 4: Around the campfire

Three friends on a camping trip share a spooky story and meet a mysterious stranger.

Ellen: Hey, guys! You're not going to believe this! I just heard a story about this campground.

Vanessa: What do you mean? What about it?

Ellen: I was just at the bathhouse. I had taken a shower and was brushing my teeth when this woman came in with her daughter. She was telling her the story, so I listened in.

Vanessa: What's so interesting about this old campground?

Molly: It isn't scary, is it? Because scary stories freak me out.

Vanessa: Oh, don't be such a chicken, Molly. Come on, Ellen, tell us the story.

Ellen: Well, this all took place many years ago. Before it was turned into a campground, this land had been a farm. It was owned by a young couple named Theodore and Dolly McShane. Mr. McShane had inherited the land from a relative.

Vanessa: So, what's so scary about that? I thought this was supposed to be a spooky story.

Ellen: I'm getting to that. Just wait. The McShanes were wonderful people: friendly, sociable. Everybody loved them. And they really, really loved each other. Everybody could see it. When they were walking down the street together, they always held hands. When he was working in the fields, he always picked her wildflowers and brought them home to her in the evening.

Vanessa: That's so sweet.

Molly: Oh, no. Then something bad happened, right?

Ellen: Yes. One day, as Theodore was coming home from town, he saw smoke in the distance. It had been a very hot, dry summer, so fires were a real danger.

Molly: Was there a fire at the farm?

Ellen: Yes! And as he was hurrying down the road, the smoke was getting thicker and thicker, blacker and blacker. All he could think about was his wife. But, by the time he got home, the house was completely in flames. He screamed Dolly's name, over and over, but she didn't answer.

Vanessa: She was in the house?

Molly: She died in the fire?

Ellen: Yes. It was a terrible tragedy.

Vanessa: What happened then?

Ellen: Well, the poor man went crazy. He refused to believe that Dolly had died. For months he searched for her. He walked all day and night, through the countryside and through the town, searching, searching. And in his hands, he always carried a bouquet of wildflowers for his poor, dead bride.

Molly: So, how did it turn out? What finally happened to him?

Ellen: That's the spooky part. It's a mystery. People saw him less and less, and then Theodore McShane just disappeared. No one ever saw him again. But the people who live here say he still walks the forest at night looking for his lost bride.

All: [*screams of surprise*]

Ranger: Oh, I'm sorry. I didn't mean to frighten you ladies. I was making my rounds and wanted to see if everything is all right.

Molly: Yes. . . . (*to friends*) A park ranger, of course. . . . (*to ranger*) Yes, everything's fine. Ellen was telling us a spooky story when you came by.

Ranger: Campfire stories, huh? That's always fun. Well, OK, then. I'll let you get back to it.

Vanessa: Thanks for checking on us. And sorry about the screams.

Ranger: That's OK. I'm used to it. Hey, in the morning you ladies should take a look down that path. There's a field full of wildflowers, and they're in bloom right now – very pretty.

Vanessa: Oh! That's good to know. We'll do that. Thanks.

Ranger: Here's some for you to enjoy. In case you need anything, I'll be at the ranger station.

Vanessa: Thanks again. Oh! What's your name?

Ranger: I'm Ted. Theodore, really, but my friends call me Ted. Ted McShane. You have a good night.

Unit 5: Travel World

Reporters around the world ask people about cross-cultural experiences.

Chris: Hi. I'm Chris Brooks. Welcome to *Travel World*. Have you ever traveled to a country with a completely different culture? If you have, you probably know what "culture shock" is. It's a feeling of confusion you get from suddenly being in a new environment. The traditions and customs may seem strange. Expectations are different. You don't know exactly what you're supposed to do. You may even be a little bit afraid of making a mistake. In time, you get used to everything. But when you get home, you often have some interesting and perhaps humorous stories to tell about your cross-cultural experiences. Today, we're going to Latin America to meet some people who've traveled abroad and hear about their experiences crossing cultures. First, let's go to Brazil.

*   *   *

Chris: Ah, yes. Rio de Janeiro. Enjoying a spectacular view of Sugar Loaf Mountain is our lucky reporter, Fátima Nolan.

Fátima: Hi, Chris. I'm here in beautiful Rio de Janeiro. Like everywhere else in the world, people here like to travel abroad and have some interesting stories to tell. Let's talk with some of them. . . . (*to Camilla*) What's your name, and where are you from?

Camilla: My name is Camilla, and I was born in Stockholm, Sweden, but I moved to Rio when I was four, and I've lived here ever since. Two years ago, I went to Sweden, and I lived there for a year.

Fátima: What did you notice that was different?

Camilla: Well, the first thing that I noticed when I got to Sweden was how people greet each other. It was completely different. Because here in Brazil, we kiss on the cheek and they shake hands. So I went to kiss like [*kissing sounds*], and they . . . "Oh, my goodness! What's going on?" And they felt like, "You're invading my space," or something like that. It was strange.

Fátima: This is Fátima Nolan from Rio de Janeiro. Back to you, Chris!

*   *   *

Chris: Thanks, Fátima. Now, let's cross the South American continent to Lima, Peru, where our reporter, Denise Arregui, is standing by. Denise?

Denise: Thanks, Chris. We're here at the beautiful Plaza de Armas. This is a favorite spot for tourists and the people of Lima. Let's talk to some people here about their cross-cultural experiences. . . . (*to Andrew*) Hi. What's your name, and where are you from?

Andrew: My name's Andrew, and I'm from the United States.

Denise: Have you noticed any differences in the way people do things here in Peru?

Andrew: Yeah. One thing that I really notice is the public transportation system is really different. Because here the bus system is private, and so there's all these people trying to get you on their bus because the way they make money is by getting as many people as possible to get on their bus. So the whole time they're yelling, "Get on my bus! Get on my bus!" And sometimes it's not the bus that you want to be getting on.

Denise: This is Denise Arregui here in Lima, Peru. Back to you, Chris.

*   *   *

Chris: Thank you, Denise. Now, reporter Hilary García is standing by in Mexico, our final destination for today. What do you have for us, Hilary?

Hilary: Thanks, Chris. I'm here in beautiful Tepoztlán, Mexico – a town that both Mexican and foreign tourists like to visit. Let's talk with a few of them about their cross-cultural experiences. . . . (*to Delfino*) Hi. What's your name, and where are you from?

Delfino: My name is Delfino Valdez, and I was born in Renosa, Mexico, and now I live in the United States.

Hilary: Tell us about your cross-cultural experience.

Delfino: I am married to an American woman. And she was making me lunch one day, and she brought me a soup and a sandwich. Once I was done with it, I said, "OK, honey. Where's the rest of it?" And she said that was it. Well, it is customary in my culture to have a huge meal in the middle of the day with the beans, the rice, a meat. So, needless to say, I was very surprised.

Hilary: This is Hilary Garcia in Tepoztlán, Mexico. Back to you, Chris.

*   *   *

Chris: Until next time, this is Chris Brooks for *Travel World*, bidding you *bon voyage*.

        Interchange 3 Video transcripts © Cambridge University Press 2012   *Photocopiable*

Unit 6: What's the problem?

A couple's hope for a relaxing weekend at a quaint hotel is dashed.

George: Norman, I've got to go to the hardware store. Room 12 really needs work.

Norman: Room 12, yeah.

George: We're expecting guests soon. So take care of them, OK?

Norman: Guests. Room 12.

George: Thanks.

         *   *   *

George: Hi.

Ed/Michelle: Hi.

Ed: Hello?

Michelle: Hello?

Ed: Anybody there?

Norman: Sorry! Hi! May I help you?

Ed: Yes. We have reservations. Quincy, Ed and Michelle, for two nights.

Norman: Yes, Mr. Quincy. You're in Room 12. May I help you with your luggage?

Michelle: Oh, no. We're OK. We're just staying two nights. We don't have a lot of luggage.

Norman: All right. Well, I'll show you the way to your room. Follow me. . . . Oh, watch that floorboard. It's loose. Be careful.

         *   *   *

Norman: Here is the temperature control. Press this button for air conditioning, this button to turn on the heat. Adjust the temperature with this dial. Bathroom's right in there. My name is Norman. Give me a call if you need anything.

Ed: He was strange. We just got here and I'm already feeling stressed out.

Michelle: Hey, does it feel cold in here to you?

Ed: Yeah. Hey, look. . . . It's stuck.

Michelle: I'm going to turn on the heat. . . . This thing's broken.

Ed: I'll call the front desk. . . . (*on phone*) Norman? We have a window that needs to be fixed, and the heat needs to be checked, too. OK, thanks. . . . (*to Michelle*) He's on his way.

Michelle: That was nice of him.

Ed: I still think he's strange. [*knocking*] That was quick.

Norman: Hi. What's the problem?

Michelle: Oh, it's cold.

Norman: Turn up the heat.

Ed: The heat doesn't work.

Norman: Well, what's wrong with it?

Michelle: The dial's broken. It came off in my hand.

Norman: That should do it.

Ed: We'll see. That window needs fixing, too. It's stuck and it's letting the cold air in.

Norman: That should do it.

Michelle: Thanks?

Norman: You're welcome.

Michelle: At least it's warming up.

Ed: Yeah, but look around. The paint is cracked and peeling. The nightstand is scratched. The curtains are torn, and the rug is worn and dirty. Actually, this place is a dump. . . . You know what? It's getting really warm in here. . . . Norman didn't fix anything. He just turned the temperature way up, and now it's stuck on high. I can't turn the heat off.

Michelle: Well, open the window.

Ed: I'm on it.

Michelle: Ed, there's no water in here.

Ed: And I can't open this window. That does it.

         *   *   *

Ed: We're leaving.

Norman: Is something the matter?

Ed: Everything's the matter! First of all, the thermostat is broken.

Michelle: It's too hot now.

Ed: And the window is stuck, and there's no water. Everything needs to be fixed. . . . (*to Michelle*) Tell me he's not strange.

Michelle: Strange? He's out of his mind.

George: Norman? . . .

Unit 7: Endangered islands

A BBC reporter explains how climate change threatens the island nation of Tuvalu.

Anchor: One of the most remote nations on Earth, threatened by rising water levels, has today experienced the damaging impact of what's known as a "king tide." Tuvalu is a small group of islands ten thousand miles and eleven time zones away, in the South Pacific. Islanders fear that the area could disappear within 50 years if action isn't taken over climate change. Well, our environment correspondent, David Shukman, has traveled to the islands, and we can join David there now.

Reporter: Thank you. It's a stormy time here in the heat of the South Pacific, just the combination of high tides and strong winds that people dread. Because Tuvalu is so low in the water, it really does run the risk of becoming the first country to fall victim to the way our climate is now changing.

*   *   *

Reporter: Incredibly beautiful, but incredibly vulnerable. The fragile strips of green that make up this country only just break the surface of the ocean. But for how much longer? The mighty waves of the Pacific pound the shoreline during what's called a "king tide" – the highest tides of the year – and the effects can be devastating. This is the island's main road.

Islander 1: I mean, we've never seen this in the past, water coming all the way up to this far. And our house is just up behind us.

Reporter: But the water also surges up from underground, through the coral the islands are built on. In the space of an hour, the lowest areas are all flooded. Everyone feels the impact. This priest steps carefully through the waters on his way to conduct a funeral. The higher the king tides get, the harder it is to keep things going here. . . . So, can you grow anything here?

Islander 2: No.

Reporter: Because it's too salty?

Islander 2: Yes, it's too salty.

Reporter: The seawater is poisoning the soil, and people are nervous.

Islander 3: It makes me feel scary [scared]. So, what will happen to us in 10 years' time?

Reporter: This isn't like other floods that I've covered, with a single catastrophic event. Instead, it's a creeping process, with this seawater flowing up into the heart of these islands, and slowly, but effectively, killing them off. . . . The water bubbles up in tiny streams and everywhere you look, it just lies on the surface. And the problem is getting worse. At the harbor, the rising swell is monitored by an Australian system. The measurements go back 15 years. And at the local Met Office, they say the king tides are getting higher, a trend forecast to continue.

Islander 4: In prediction, the next five to ten years, the king tide [is] getting worse and it [is] getting higher than normal. Then most of the coastal areas will be wash [washed] out.

Reporter: The implications are alarming. A typical high tide reaches about two and a half meters. A king tide, like now, could be more than three. The U.N. climate panel forecast the rise of another half meter, when the highest point is only about four and a half meters. Now for Tuvalu, each scenario would cost precious land. Only a small rise would see parts of the island go under, perhaps even the runway: a lifeline to the outside world. . . . How long have you got?

Islander 5: Not more than 50 years. In fact, some of the islands have already disappeared. Please, help us! You cause climate change. You know the "polluter pays" principle must apply. You must give, . . . set up a global fund to which these islands can come and tap into, to build their resilience, to build their capacity, their education, technology, and all that – and restore what damage has been done.

Reporter: People here say there must be a technological fix, if a rich country like Dubai can build entirely new islands, especially since these are so narrow you can cross from one side to the other in a few short paces. The problem: they're founded on coral, which is porous. Saving these islands will cost a fortune. . . . For the children of Tuvalu, the floods are fun. But for them to lead their lives on these islands will require massive international support. And with just 11,000 people here, will the outside world think it's worth it?

*   *   *

Interchange 3 Video transcripts © Cambridge University Press 2012   Photocopiable

Reporter: Now, of course, Tuvalu does get some aid, but not nearly enough to keep the rising sea at bay. So the international community faces very soon a difficult choice of whether to draw a line between those who get saved and those who don't. And in the meantime, people here are getting ready for another king tide. Right now it's low; it's due to get very high in about eight hours' time. Back to you in the studio.

Anchor: David, thank you very much. David Shukman there, our environment correspondent, in Tuvalu.

Unit 8: Tango!

A reporter talks to several people about learning to dance the tango.

Kevin: From ballet to ballroom, and salsa to swing, learning to dance is one of today's hottest trends. And tango dancing is the hottest of them all. Tango fever has spread all over the world. Hi, I'm Kevin Kaine. And once a month, people come here to the Weeks Bridge in Cambridge, Massachusetts, to learn tango. . . . (*to the couple*) Hi, how's your tango lesson going?

Woman 1: Oh, it's super fun!

Kevin: So, why did you decide to take a tango class?

Woman 1: I was just interested in dancing.

Man 1: And a lot of our friends come here.

Kevin: What's the best way to improve your dancing?

Woman 1: Just by going to a tango club.

Man 1: And by practicing hard.

Woman 1: True.

* * *

Kevin: How did you learn to dance?

Man 2: By coming to class.

Kevin: And why did you decide to take tango lessons?

Man 2: Because I wanted to keep fit and have fun at the same time.

* * *

Woman 2: Well, I took some lessons, and I come here to practice.

Kevin: So what's a good way to improve your dancing?

Woman 2: By practicing with a guy. But you have to find a good partner!

* * *

Kevin: Now we're going to talk to a tango instructor, Uche. . . . (*to Uche*) Hi.

Uche: Hi.

Kevin: Why do you think tango is so popular?

Uche: I think tango is popular because it's very exotic and it's also very challenging for people, and once people learn something that they find challenging and it's very exotic, I think they feel very rewarded. [*dance instruction in background*: . . . step six, back, collect, . . . seven, . . . and then instead of collecting, you actually switch your weight. . . .]

Kevin: What do you recommend for people who want to learn tango?

Uche: I would recommend starting with group classes or private classes.

Kevin: And after you've learned the basics of tango, what's a good way to improve your moves?

Uche: By going out dancing with the people that you've taken the lessons with, practicing at home, listening to the music, . . . just feeling very comfortable with the music, . . . and then going out dancing again.

* * *

Kevin: How long have you been coming here?

Man 2: I've been coming here for about six years.

Kevin: Why?

Man 2: Because I love tango.

Kevin: And what is it about tango that you love so much?

Man 2: I think it's got a great rhythm. I think it's got passion. It's a fun type of dance.

Kevin: Do you have any advice for people who want to learn to tango?

Man 2: A lot of people don't think they can dance until they get out here and try it. I think dancing starts by taking the initiative. Take a class.

* * *

Kevin: Do you prefer taking lessons in a studio or going out somewhere like this?

Woman 2: I prefer going out and dancing. There's a different energy; it's more social. But there's nothing wrong with taking lessons. I recommend it.

Kevin: Why do you think tango is so popular?

Woman 2: You can grow into it. You let your body move to the music and you create a dance with someone. And it's relaxing, once you learn it.

Kevin: Do you have any advice for people who want to learn tango?

Woman 2: It depends on how you learn. Some people learn best by taking classes. I learn best by watching and listening to the music and then getting brave and trying it a little. You know, learn by doing and practicing.

* * *

Kevin: OK, I'm ready to take the plunge. How do I get started?

Woman 3: It's not too difficult. Take this arm up behind my back. This one up. Now just start walking. That's perfect. Try a step to the side. Good. Then a step back. Now side again.

Kevin: Hey, this is a lot of fun! You should try it. This is Kevin, actually dancing tango, from the Weeks Bridge in Cambridge, Massachusetts.

Unit 9: Stressed out

A woman seeks advice from a co-worker on how to relieve stress.

Carmen: (*on phone*) Hello? . . . Yes, Pat. I'm working on that right now. . . . Uh huh. . . . OK. . . . By five o'clock. . . . Yes. OK. Thanks.

Hugo: What's up, Carmen? You look really stressed out.

Carmen: It's this job, Hugo. I'm constantly under pressure. My muscles are tense. My neck is stiff. My stomach is in knots. I just . . . I can't seem to relax.

Hugo: Yeah, stress is a killer. One thing you could do is get some exercise. It's a great way to relieve tension.

Carmen: I tried that.

Hugo: Did it help?

Carmen: It's a long story. First, I tried skating.

Hugo: I love skating. How'd it work out?

Carmen: It didn't.

Hugo: I'll say.

Carmen: Then I tried dance lessons.

Hugo: Oh, I love dancing.

Carmen: Me, too. And so does my husband, but . . .

Hugo: But?

Carmen: He was a little too . . . enthusiastic.

Hugo: Aha. Well, have you thought about taking a yoga class? They say it's very relaxing.

Carmen: Yoga, relaxing? Are you kidding me? You see this paper clip?

Hugo: Yes.

Carmen: This is what I'd look like after my yoga class.

Hugo: Ouch! There's always hypnotherapy.

Carmen: I've tried that, too. Now, every time I hear the word "ocean," it's supposed to relax me. Oh, and it works! The other day, I was in a meeting. Someone started talking about the environmental problems in the world's oceans. People said the word "ocean" so many times, I fell asleep.

Hugo: Oh, yeah. I heard about that. That must've been embarrassing.

Carmen: Now half the office knows. . . . [*coworker yawns loudly*] See what I mean? I need to get the hypnotherapy reversed.

Hugo: I have an idea. You could try aromatherapy.

Carmen: What's that?

Hugo: It's like a massage, but they rub your skin with scented oils.

Carmen: Um, I'm not sure about that. I'm allergic to perfume.

Hugo: Well, it might be a good idea, then, for you to take some time off. Go on vacation. Rent a little house on the beach or something. You know, . . . on the ocean.

Carmen: The ocean? [*yawns*] That's a good idea. Maybe I'll take a vacation.

Hugo: It's very relaxing, lying on the beach, listening to the sounds of the ocean.

Carmen: [*yawns more*]

Hugo: Ocean . . . ocean. . . . Enjoy your vacation.

Unit 10: The Virtual Office

ABC News presents a report on the changing face of the workplace.

Anchor: Finally from us, the virtual office. For better or worse, technology and globalization are creating startling changes in what it means to be "on the job." Betsey Stark is tracking the new order of business and tonight begins our series, "The Future of Work."

*   *   *

Reporter: Imagine a work world with no commute, no corporate headquarters, maybe no office in the physical world at all. For Bob Flavin, Janet Hoffman, and Joseph Jaffe, the future is already here.

Bob Flavin: These days we do so much stuff by teleconferences and things, um, that it doesn't matter where you are.

Reporter: Like 42 percent of IBM's 350,000 employees, Bob Flavin rarely comes in to an IBM office.

Dan Pelino: We don't care where and how you get your work done. We care that you get your work done.

Reporter: On the day we met him, he was collaborating with computer scientists in British Columbia and Beijing from the on-call room of his local ambulance corps, where he works as a volunteer.

Receptionist: *(background)* You are in six-zero-three-one.

Reporter: The workforce at the Accenture management consulting firm is so mobile, not even the CEO has an office with his name on the door. . . . *(interview)* There's no corporate headquarters?

Janet Hoffman: No.

Reporter: *(report)* If you need a workspace, you reserve it like a hotel room, checking in and out at a kiosk.

Janet Hoffman: Having a big desk is a sign of status, with lots of family photos and, uh, you know, and carpeting that's fluffy and nice is, uh, that is a vision of the past.

Male voice: *(background)* Come on in to the theater.

Reporter: In the future, more companies with scattered workforces and clients may do what the Crayon marketing firm has done and make their headquarters in cyberspace.

Joseph Jaffe: Here's our little rooftop. We had our holiday party here.

Reporter: Crayon's workers rarely meet in the physical world, . . .

Man 1: I am, uh, in Boston today.

Man 2: And I am on Long Island today.

Reporter: . . . but their alter egos in the virtual world gather once a week.

Joseph Jaffe: We're here in, uh, in our boardroom, and you're here actually at the tail end of a status meeting.

Reporter: I never met Crayon's CEO in person, . . . *(background)* There you are. . . . *(report)* but we spent a couple of hours together in cyberspace.

Joseph Jaffe: Our belief is that if we bring like minds together, no matter where they are in the world, we can actually create that connectedness as if we're actually here at the same place at the same time.

Reporter: If what matters is what you do, not where you are, who needs an office? Betsey Stark, ABC News, Crayonville, in cyberspace.

*   *   *

Anchor: And tomorrow, imagine having summers off . . . every summer! That is *World News* for this Monday. I'm Kate Snow. For Charles Gibson and all of us at ABC News, have a good evening. Good night.

Interchange 3 Video transcripts © Cambridge University Press 2012   Photocopiable

Unit 11: Live and learn

A host asks people to share embarrassing stories.

Jamie Fitch: Hi, I'm Jamie Fitch. Today we're going to hear from some people about their most embarrassing moments. Our first guest is Amber McCarthy.... (*to Amber*) Welcome, Amber.

Amber: Thank you.

Jamie: What do you do?

Amber: I work at an advertising agency.

Jamie: Really? Interesting. Could you tell us about an embarrassing moment you've had?

Amber: Well, right after college, I got my job at the agency. At the end of the first week, my supervisor called me into a meeting with an important client. The moment I walked in they stopped talking and looked at me. I looked so unprofessional! It was so embarrassing. I realized I was the only one not wearing a suit. I looked like I was still in college. I should have asked about office dress codes.

Jamie: Yes, but you dress very professionally now.

Amber: Live and learn.

Jamie: Thanks for sharing that story with us.

Amber: Sure.

*   *   *

Jamie: Now I'm speaking with Evan Kim.... (*to Evan*) Evan, what do you do?

Evan: I work for a technology company.

Jamie: What's the most embarrassing thing that's ever happened to you?

Evan: I was attending a conference out of town and staying with an old friend, Ed, and his family.

*   *   *

All: Hi! Good to see you!

Michelle: (*upstairs*) Ben! ... (*to Evan*) So nice to finally meet you. Hi! I'm Michelle! Come on in!

Evan: Nice to meet you.

*   *   *

Evan: The first morning, I overslept. I was rushing to leave the house ... when I knocked over a vase and broke it. No one was awake yet, and I was in a hurry, so I just threw away the pieces. By the time I had cleaned it up, I was really late, so I left. I should have called Ed and told him about it, but, honestly, I forgot. That night, when I got back to the house, Ed and his wife, Michelle, were having an argument with their son, Ben. They thought Ben had broken the vase and then tried to hide it. Ben kept saying he hadn't done it, but no one believed him. As soon as I realized what they were arguing about, I told them I was the one that broke the vase.

*   *   *

Ed: (*to Ben*) OK, you need to step forward, and take ownership ...

Evan: Guys, ... guys, please ...

Ed: (*to Evan*) Please, this is family business ...

Evan: Ed, please, just ... just stop.... I broke the vase.

*   *   *

Evan: I was so embarrassed. I had broken a vase *and* caused an argument.

Jamie: Oh, no. Well, what should you have done?

Evan: I should have left a note, or called, or something. I offered to buy a new vase, but Michelle didn't want that. It turns out the vase was a family heirloom and very special to her. If I had known that, I would have woken her up and told her about it when it happened.

*   *   *

Evan: Michelle, I'm sorry. Ben, I'm sorry.

*   *   *

Evan: She forgave me, but her son still won't talk to me.

Jamie: He will eventually.

Evan: I hope so. Maybe I should have bought him something to apologize.

Jamie: Thanks for the story, Evan.

*   *   *

Jamie: And now let's talk with Alexis Reynolds.... (*to Alexis*) Welcome.

Alexis: Thank you.

Jamie: What do you do, Alexis?

Alexis: I'm a student, and I also work part-time at a theater.

Jamie: What's your most embarrassing moment?

Alexis: I was taking tickets at the theater. There were all these really famous actors. Everybody was there. It was a very important performance. One of the reasons that I work at the theater is so I can see the plays for free. So after I'm finished taking tickets, I can go sit in the back and watch the play. And, so I was sitting there, and I was totally into it, and the audience was just spellbound. And right at the most dramatic moment of the play, ... [*cell phone ringtone*] my cell phone rang.

Jamie: Oh, my gosh!

Alexis: Just wait, it gets so much worse. Um, so, my

ringtone is hip-hop, and it was turned all the way up. I mean really loud. And of course, I couldn't find my phone in my bag. So, by the time I finally found the phone, everybody was staring at me. It seemed like an eternity. I pretty much wanted to crawl under my seat and hide. I am so glad that my boss wasn't there that night, because if he had been, I would have been fired.

Jamie: Well, that sounds awful. But you've recovered.

Alexis: Yeah, I have recovered. But from now on, my cell phone is on "vibrate."

Jamie: Yeah, good idea.

*   *   *

Jamie: What's the most embarrassing thing that's ever happened to *you*?

Unit 12: Good business

A student interviews a local business owner about her secrets of success.

Jacob: Hi. This is Jacob with Campus TV. Today we're at Choice Café on University Drive. I'm talking to the owner, Lili Chen. Choice Café opened two years ago. Since then, students have been lining up for coffee and food. Why is Choice Café so successful? Let's find out. . . . (*interview*) Thank you for agreeing to speak with me today. Choice Café is popular on campus.

Lili: Yes, the café is doing very well.

Jacob: What's the secret to your success?

Lili: I've been very lucky. And I have great customers. But it is hard. I think there are several reasons we do so well. We're popular because of our location, of course. For a café to succeed, it can't be off the beaten path. It needs to be where people can find it.

Jacob: You don't have to walk far. It's convenient – right next to campus. But that can't be the only reason. After all, Central Café closed last year, and it was just one block away from campus. Did Choice put Central Café out of business?

Lili: Yes and no. We were definitely in competition with each other. But Central Café didn't have comfortable seats. In order for a café to attract customers, it should have comfortable chairs. Our café is famous for its cozy atmosphere. Look at those chairs. People can come here to relax, drink their tea or coffee, and study or read.

Jacob: Do you encourage people to stay a long time?

Lili: I absolutely do encourage people to stay. I think that's the reason why they keep coming back. They can read, do homework, meet their friends. And during this time they drink two or three cups of coffee and have a pastry.

Jacob: What about the food?

Lili: Our food is made here fresh every morning. We have a strong take-out business. People order food to take home or to eat outside.

Jacob: Outside? You mean, on the grass, on campus?

Lili: Anywhere. We do have tables outside, too. But people do eat on campus. It's really pretty there.

Jacob: But it's nice to sit inside, too. The atmosphere is great here. Talk about that for a minute: the lights, the music.

Lili: Music is key to a café's success. You need to make sure you have good music. I'm not an expert. I mean, I don't know much about music. But people who work here are students. They're tuned in. They know what's popular. So I let them choose the music.

Jacob: And people like it.

Lili: Yes. And since I want to encourage people to meet their friends here, chat, read, so on, I make sure the music's not too loud. I mean, we can hear each other just fine, right?

Jacob: Right. Well, Lili, thank you. I've really enjoyed learning more about what makes Choice a successful café.

Lili: You're welcome, Jacob. Come anytime!

Jacob: For Campus TV, this is Jacob, signing off.

Interchange 3 Video transcripts © Cambridge University Press 2012   Photocopiable

Unit 13: Stonehenge

The History Channel presents current scientific theories on the mysterious origin and purpose of Stonehenge.

Narrator: Stonehenge is a mysterious ancient monument, isolated deep in the English countryside. To this day, no one has been able to determine who built Stonehenge, or why. The original monument was made up of approximately 153 colossal standing stones, weighing up to 40 tons, and arranged in a circular enclosure.

John Rennie: The people who built Stonehenge must have been doing so for purposes that seemed very, very important to them at the time. It was always a literally monumental undertaking. A lot of the big stones come from Wales, so transporting those, for people who didn't have the wheel, has to have been an unbelievably difficult undertaking.

Narrator: Stonehenge has been called everything from a Neolithic hospital to an alien landing site; a solar temple to a Druid shrine.

Julian Richards: The period we're dealing with here is our prehistory, and what defines prehistory is that we've got no written records about anything. So everything that we understand about it comes from archaeology, from what we can excavate and what we can analyze.

Narrator: In 2008, hundreds of human bones were excavated at the site, primitively burned and buried. The bones were dated across a thousand years of prehistory.

Julian Richards: The first analysis of all the cremated bones that were found at Stonehenge suggests that it's mainly adult males, . . . adult men that were buried there. So it's quite a distinctive group of people, and only probably very important people came there to be buried.

Narrator: The cremated remains suggest that the history books may need to be rewritten. Stonehenge could have been a temple of the dead, a place where ancient people came to commune with the spirits. And the 2009 discovery of a second circle, called Blue Stonehenge, appears to be further evidence that Stonehenge formed part of a huge ceremonial complex.

Julian Richards: Stonehenge clearly is a place of ceremonies. It's a place where people gathered together. I don't think they built it and then just abandoned it. And I'm sure that elaborate ceremonies went on there.

Narrator: It is these rituals and ceremonies that are key to understanding a people lost to history.

Unit 14: Making music

A look at how a song is written, is produced, and gets played on the air.

Matthew: My name is Matthew Hawkes and I'm a singer/songwriter. Making music is my creative outlet: the way I make sense of the world around me. When I sit down to compose, the first thing I do is tune my guitar. Once the guitar is tuned up and ready, I set up the keyboard. The keyboard has multiple functions and multiple sounds. What comes out of me is a reflection of how I'm feeling that day. Sometimes I can spend hours writing one piece. I'm writing this song. I titled it "Revelations." . . . [*singing in background*] . . . When I sit down to write, one of the things I like to use most is a thesaurus. I started with the one word, "revelations." I look it up in a thesaurus, and I could have ten words, then – each with a different sound, each offering a different rhyme scheme for me.

*   *   *

Matthew: (*singing*) . . . rise like the sun, through the sky, and when it's done, I will think about all that's true. At the end of the day, if I don't get my way, I will wake knowing what to do . . .

*   *   *

Matthew: When I feel I've taken my song as far as I can, I then bring it to a recording studio. I think it's important to get feedback and ideas from other musicians. Aldous Collins is a guitarist and a friend. He accompanies me in the recording studio. At the studio, we work with a recording engineer.

Richard: I'm Richard Marr. I'm a recording engineer. My job is to capture music of a band. I go around and mike everything up. It comes through my board, and it's recorded into the computer system here – a multitrack recorder. . . . (*to musicians*) All right, guys. Rolling. One, two, three, . . .

Matthew: The recording engineer mixes all the vocals and instruments together. Recording your music can actually teach you a lot. You hear your own music differently. It changes your perspective, and you notice all kinds of things that you didn't when you composed the song.

*   *   *

Matthew/Aldous: (*singing*) . . . At the end of the day, if I don't get my way, I will wake knowing what to do, . . . wake knowing what to do . . .

*   *   *

Matthew: At the end of the recording session, I have a digital file of my song. I take my songs to radio stations and try to get them to play them on the air, to build an audience for my song and my music.

*   *   *

Melanie: Hi, my name's Melanie Oliver. I'm the program director here at the radio station. The program director's job is to decide what music is played on air. So I pick the songs and tell the DJs what songs to play. . . . (*to DJ*) Hi, Josh. Come on in.

Josh: Hey, Melanie.

Melanie: Hey. So I've picked the three songs that we're going to use for the local music show. OK, here's some background information.

Josh: Great.

Melanie: One of the artist's names is Matthew Hawkes. The song is called "Revelations." It's going to be a really good song, so I think you should play it on your show.

Josh: Great. I look forward to playing it.

Melanie: Great. Thank you.

Josh: Thank you.

*   *   *

Josh: My name is Josh McBride, and I'm a DJ right here at the radio station. The main responsibility of a DJ is to play music on the radio. Other responsibilities include adjusting the volume, speaking with listeners, conducting contests, and reading commercials. . . . (*on air*) Here's a new one from a Boston local. Matthew Hawkes did this one. This is "Revelations," right here on W-E-R-S.

*   *   *

        Interchange 3 Video transcripts © *Cambridge University Press 2012   Photocopiable*

Matthew: And now, people all over the world
can download it, too, which is so cool.
If you want to download it, look me up.
My name is Matt Hawkes at
www.matthawkes.com. And the song
is "Revelations." Enjoy!

Lyrics:

Revelations
Revelations, spinning 'round.
Turned a corner, so profound.
I'm sick of this room without a view.
These people don't know me like I think they do.

I will rise like the sun, through the sky, and when it's done, will think about all that's true.
At the end of the day, if I don't get my way, I will wake knowing what to do, wake knowing what to do.

I will rise, rise like the sun.
I will rise, rise like the sun.

Rise like the sun, through the sky and when it's done, will think about all that's true.
At the end of the day, if I don't get my way, I will wake knowing what to do, wake knowing what to do.

Unit 15: The streets of Montreal

A reporter in Montreal, Quebec, Canada, interviews people about bicycling in the city.

Reporter: Hi. I'm Kai Nagata. I'm a television journalist based here in Montreal, Canada, and I'm also a life-long cyclist. Right now, cycling is getting more and more popular in Montreal, with 10 percent of all commuters getting to work by bike, like me. And city officials want that number to increase. More bicycles means more bicycle traffic, and that means sharing the road. There's lots of opinions about how pedestrians, cyclists, and drivers should act and interact in the city. Let's find out what people think.

*　　　　*　　　　*

Reporter: Is there anything Montreal could do to improve things for cyclists?

Sebastian: Yeah, well, I think the city should try to expand the system of cycle paths. One thing I learned this morning is that one shouldn't drive against traffic because that's a problem. Sometimes there are corners where drivers just cannot see you coming, and so you should really try to avoid driving against the traffic, if possible.

*　　　　*　　　　*

Reporter: What advice do you have for cyclists in the city?

Nitai: Cyclists should have their own bike lane and drive towards the oncoming traffic because they will be able to better see what the other parked cars are doing, . . . whether they're driving or parked, the cyclist will have more control.

Reporter: What do you think drivers ought to do to help keep cyclists safe?

Nitai: Drivers should always check their rearview mirrors before opening their doors, so that they don't hit a bicycle that's coming up behind them.

*　　　　*　　　　*

Reporter: Do you spend more time driving or riding a bike?

Marina: Driving.

Reporter: What do you think Montreal could do to encourage cycling as an option for people?

Marina: Maybe education. Maybe some restrictions to driving downtown.

Reporter: So maybe making it harder for drivers . . .

Marina: Right, right. That's the nature, the human nature.

*　　　　*　　　　*

Reporter: What advice would you give people who are cycling with children?

Susan: There should be a law that says all children starting from age 6, should be educated on the rules of bicycling.

Reporter: What do you think of the idea of kids wearing bike helmets?

Susan: I think they should, but a lot of them won't.

*　　　　*　　　　*

Reporter: What do you think the city could do to make cyclists even safer in Montreal?

Denise: I think it would be best if bicycles and buses were not on the same street.

Reporter: Why do you think that?

Denise: Because they're not compatible. The bus is very large, and we're very small and not protected, but we drive approximately the same speed, or in the same path.

*　　　　*　　　　*

Reporter: What do you think cyclists should do to help keep themselves safe in traffic?

Christopher: Be more aware of both automobiles and pedestrians. I think there are ways in which sometimes we cut corners in terms of moving through traffic – particularly moving traffic. I think cyclists need to be aware.

Reporter: What do you think when you see cyclists riding around with headphones in?

Christopher: I don't think it's the best idea. You have to be alert. You don't often need your ears when you're cycling, but every once in a while, you hear something that indicates something that you didn't see. And, for safety reasons, that, I think, you know, . . . I'd like to bike and listen to music, too, but if you're going to do that, I think you should do that in a park.

*　　　　*　　　　*

Reporter: What advice do you have for cyclists in the city?

Cai: People should never wear Walkmans or iPods or whatever while they cycle, because a lot of cycle safety has to do with listening.

Reporter: What advice would you give people who are cycling with children?

Cai: I think cycling on the sidewalk is fine, with kids. I think most pedestrians are at ease with it. You know, look here: look at how wide this

　　　Interchange 3 Video transcripts © Cambridge University Press 2012　Photocopiable

sidewalk is. If you have young children who are just learning to cycle, I don't see anything wrong with cycling on the sidewalk along here.

Reporter: What's your impression of Montreal as a city for cycling?

Cai: Cyclists should take a bigger piece of the city and play a bigger role in the city. And I think that drivers and even pedestrians should relax a bit about cyclists. Cyclists are good for cities.

       *   *   *

Reporter: Wherever bikes and cars share the road, people are going to have opinions about how they ought to interact. Montreal is no exception. And we may not have solved all the problems yet, but we're working on it. I'm Kai Nagata, reporting from Montreal, Quebec, Canada.

Unit 16: The Harlem Children's Zone

An interview with Geoffrey Canada, an education reformer in the U.S., excerpted from the CBS News program 60 Minutes.

Anchor: Now CNN's Anderson Cooper on assignment for *60 Minutes*.

*   *   *

Reporter: For years, educators have tried and failed to get poor kids from the inner city to do just as well in school as kids from America's more affluent suburbs. Black kids still routinely score well below white kids on national standardized tests. But a man named Geoffrey Canada may have figured out a way to close that racial achievement gap. What he's doing has been called one of the most ambitious social experiments to alleviate poverty of our lifetime. His laboratory is a 97-block neighborhood in Harlem, which he's flooded with a wide array of social, medical, and educational services available for free to the 10,000 children who live there. It's called the Harlem Children's Zone. Ed Bradley first reported on Geoffrey Canada three and a half years ago, but back then there was no way to tell if his Children's Zone was working. Today, however, results are in and they're nothing short of stunning, so much so that the White House is now taking notice. For Geoffrey Canada, however, it's just a start.

*   *   *

Canada: You grow up in America and you're told from day one, this is the land of opportunity, that everybody has an equal chance to make it in this country. And then you look at places like Harlem, and you say that is absolutely a lie.

Reporter: So you're trying to level the playing field between kids here in Harlem and, what, middle-class kids in a suburb?

Canada: That's exactly what we think we have to do. You know, if you grow up in a community where your schools are inferior, where the sounds of gunshots are a common thing, where you spend your time and energy not thinking about algebra or geometry, but about how not to get beat up, or not to get shot, or not to get raped. When you grow up like that, you don't have the same opportunity as other children growing up. And we're trying to change those odds.

Reporter: He's trying to change those odds on a scale never before attempted. His goal: to break the cycle of poverty in an entire neighborhood by making sure all the kids who live there go to college. . . . [*singing*] . . . You really believe that's possible, to break that cycle?

Canada: I absolutely know we're going to do it.

Reporter: Canada remembers well what it was like to be a kid in the inner city. He grew up not far from Harlem in another tough New York neighborhood: the South Bronx. Abandoned by his father, he and his three brothers were raised by their mother, who was barely able to get by.

Canada: When I first found out that Superman wasn't real, I was about, maybe, eight, and I was talking to my mother about it. And she was like, "No, no, no, there's no Superman." And I started crying. The chaos, the violence, the danger. No hero was coming.

Reporter: Canada got lucky, however. As a teenager, his grandparents moved to the suburbs and he went with them. He got into Bowdoin College and then the Harvard School of Education.

Canada: Good morning, boys and girls.

Reporter: He's been working with kids in Harlem virtually ever since. . . . [*singing*] . . . To do it, Geoffrey Canada decided to build his own school in the Harlem Children's Zone. Right now, there are some twelve hundred [1,200] kids enrolled from kindergarten to the tenth grade. It'll eventually expand all the way through the twelfth grade.

Canada: We've created a school to help you all become the smartest boys and girls in the country.

Reporter: It's a charter school, so Canada is able to run it his way, free from the bureaucracy and restrictions of the public school system. There's one adult for every six students, classes are smaller, and school days longer. Kids come in on Saturdays, and summer vacation – that only lasts three weeks.

Teacher 1: We will always ask permission before leaving the group?

Boy: Yes.

Reporter: Canada's long argued that investing in the Harlem Children's Zone would show a return, and now, for the first time, there's scientific data to prove it.

Dr. Fryer: He has done a remarkable job.

Reporter: Dr. [Doctor] Roland Fryer is a professor in the economics department at Harvard. He has conducted the first independent statistical study of Geoffrey Canada's efforts to close the racial achievement gap in his school.

Reporter: What . . . what is the racial achievement gap?

Dr. Fryer: Black children in our schools are not performing at even close the rate as white children in our schools. The average black 17-year-old reads at the proficiency level of the average white 13-year-old. A four-year difference in effective reading skills: that's . . . that's huge.

Reporter: But when Dr. Fryer analyzed four years' worth of Promise Academy test scores, he discovered something remarkable.

Dr. Fryer: At the elementary school level, he closed the achievement gap in both subjects: math and reading.

Reporter: Actually eliminating the gap in elementary school?

Dr. Fryer: Absolutely. We've never seen . . . we've never seen anything like that. Absolutely eliminating the gap. The gap is gone, and that is absolutely incredible.

Reporter: Last year, according to New York State data, a hundred percent of Canada's third-graders scored at or above grade level in math . . .

Teacher 2: Good job.

Reporter: . . . narrowly outperforming their white peers in the city's public schools.

Teacher 3: Ninety-six. Is that the answer?

Students: Yes.

Reporter: Even more impressive, Canada's impact on middle schoolers: kids who enrolled in the Promise Academy in the sixth grade. They started out far behind grade level, but Dr. Fryer found that within three years they had virtually eliminated the achievement gap in math and reduced it by nearly half in reading.

Dr. Fryer: These are kids that a lot of people had given up on. And he showed that it's never too late.

Reporter: How will you know when the Children's Zone has worked?

Canada: When I see my kids by the thousands with degrees. I will say this is what we set out to do, and we've done it. We've got our kids in the best schools in America. They're going to be successful. They'll be competing with everybody else all over the country. People will be looking for kids from Harlem, saying, "Oh, those kids are so great from Harlem. We need more kids from Harlem to come in." Then, we'll be successful.

Bonus track: The Harlem Children's Zone

The full interview with Geoffrey Canada, an education reformer in the U.S., from the CBS News program 60 Minutes.

Anchor: Now CNN's Anderson Cooper on assignment for *60 Minutes*.

* * *

Reporter: For years, educators have tried and failed to get poor kids from the inner city to do just as well in school as kids from America's more affluent suburbs. Black kids still routinely score well below white kids on national standardized tests. But a man named Geoffrey Canada may have figured out a way to close that racial achievement gap. What he's doing has been called one of the most ambitious social experiments to alleviate poverty of our lifetime. His laboratory is a 97-block neighborhood in Harlem, which he's flooded with a wide array of social, medical, and educational services available for free to the 10,000 children who live there. It's called the Harlem Children's Zone. Ed Bradley first reported on Geoffrey Canada three and a half years ago, but back then there was no way to tell if his Children's Zone was working. Today, however, results are in and they are nothing short of stunning, so much so that the White House is now taking notice. For Geoffrey Canada, however, it's just a start.

* * *

Canada: You grow up in America and you're told from day one, this is the land of opportunity, that everybody has an equal chance to make it in this country. And then you look at places like Harlem, and you say that is absolutely a lie.

Reporter: So you're trying to level the playing field between kids here in Harlem and, what, middle-class kids in a suburb?

Canada: That's exactly what we think we have to do. You know if you grow up in a community where your schools are inferior, where the sounds of gunshots are a common thing, where you spend your time and energy not thinking about algebra or geometry, but about how not to get beat up, or not to get shot, or not to get raped. When you grow up like that, you don't have the same opportunity as other children growing up. And we're trying to change those odds.

Reporter: He's trying to change those odds on a scale never before attempted. His goal: to break the cycle of poverty in an entire neighborhood by making sure all the kids who live there go to college. . . . [*singing*] . . . You really believe that's possible, to break that cycle?

Canada: I absolutely know we're going to do it.

Reporter: Canada remembers well what it was like to be a kid in the inner city.

Canada: We couldn't afford . . .

Reporter: He grew up not far from Harlem in another tough New York neighborhood, the South Bronx. Abandoned by his father, he and his three brothers were raised by their mother, who was barely able to get by.

Canada: When I first found out that Superman wasn't real, I was about, maybe, eight, and I was talking to my mother about it. And she was like, "No, no, no, there's no Superman." And I started crying. The chaos, the violence, the danger. No hero was coming.

Reporter: Canada got lucky, however. As a teenager, his grandparents moved to the suburbs and he went with them. He got into Bowdoin College and then the Harvard School of Education.

Canada: Good morning, boys and girls.

Reporter: He's been working with kids in Harlem virtually ever since.

Canada: You know, one of the first things kids ask me when they really get to know me, they say, "Mr. Canada." I say, "Yes, sir." "Are you rich?" And I say, "Yeah, I am." And they're so excited because they think, "I finally know somebody who has power." What they really want to ask is, "Is there any way that you can help me figure out how to get a nice car and maybe get a house?" And I think they want someone to say, "Yes, you can. I got out, you can get out. There's a way. And I'm going to help you do that."

Reporter: [*children singing*] . . . To do it, Geoffrey Canada decided to build his own school in the Harlem Children's Zone. Right now, there are some twelve hundred [1,200] kids enrolled from kindergarten to the tenth grade. It'll eventually expand all the way through the twelfth grade.

Canada: We've created a school to help you all become the smartest boys and girls in the country.

Reporter: It's a charter school, so Canada is able to run it his way, free from the bureaucracy and restrictions of the public school system. There's one adult for every six students, classes are smaller, and school days longer. Kids come in on Saturdays, and summer vacation – that only lasts three weeks.

Teacher 1: We will always ask permission before leaving the group?

Boy: Yes.

Teacher 1: OK.

Reporter: Discipline is strict and so is the dress code. To teach kids healthy eating habits, there are cooking classes using ingredients from the school's own organic garden. And if any of the kids get sick, this onsite clinic provides free medical, mental health, and even dental care. Canada calls his school the Promise Academy, and this is what he tells parents at the start of each year.

Canada: We promise our families, if your children are with us, we guarantee they're going to get into college and we're going to stick with them through college, right? . . . So that's . . . that's a promise.

Reporter: How can you, though, actually promise that they will go to college?

Canada: If my kids don't go to college, people who work for me are losing their jobs. And there's just no way around that.

Reporter: You'll fire the teachers.

Canada: I will. I will fire the teachers. I'll fire the . . . the . . . the afterschool workers. I'll fire the directors. Everybody understands that this thing is our job as the adult. And we're not going to hold the kids responsible, right? And . . . and are some of my kids belligerent? Yes. Do some of them come in and don't try hard? Yes, they do. Do they come from broken homes? Yes. Is there poverty and drugs and crime? Yes, it's all those things. Those kids are still going to college.

Richar: My name is Richar Anozier.

Reporter: Richar Anozier wasn't too sure about college when Ed Bradley first met him back in 2005. He was just in kindergarten.

Reporter 2: You want to go to college?

Richar: Much as it kills me, yes.

Reporter 2: Much as it kills you. Why was it . . . would it kill you to go into college?

Richar: Because they got . . . because they got, um, people . . . words that I don't know.

Reporter 2: But you'll learn new words every year. Trust me, you'll be OK.

Richar: OK.

Reporter: Today, Richar is in the fifth grade and seems a lot more confident about college. Do you know what college you want to go to?

Richar: Stanford.

Reporter: What do you want to do after Stanford?

Richar: I would like to earn my way to being a CEO.

Reporter: Why do you want to be the CEO?

Richar: To tell you the truth, I think you get paid better when you're CEO.

Reporter: I think you're right.

Canada: If you work hard . . .

Reporter: To make sure his kids succeed, Geoffrey Canada will do just about anything.

Canada: Who in this group went to Disney World this summer?

Reporter: For younger students who ace their statewide tests, there are free trips. And he pays high-schoolers up to a hundred and twenty dollars [$120] a month if they get near-perfect attendance and grades. . . . (to Canada) Aren't you kind of basically bribing them?

Canada: I love to bribe kids.

Reporter: (laughing) You love to bribe kids.

Canada: You know, I love to bribe . . . because this is . . . look, people say, "Well, Geoff, don't you want kids to do it for the intrinsic value of it?" Sure, I'd love them to do it for the intrinsic value. And until then, I'd love them to do it for money. I don't care. I just want them to do it!

Students: There are no excuses.

Reporter: Tuition at the Promise Academy is free, but there's not enough room for all the kids who live in the zone. So admission is by lottery.

Canada: So let me tell you how this lottery is going to go.

Reporter: This August, we watched as anxious parents waited to hear if their children would get in.

Woman 1: Drew Roberts.

Reporter: There were 210 slots open for a new kindergarten class, but 375 kids had applied.

Woman 1: Tyler Fibbs. Phillip Canti deFoex.

Reporter: As the slots filled up, some parents left waiting began to realize that their child's chances of success in life had just been reduced.

Woman 2: There are three-year-old children, and their brain is just starting to develop.

Reporter: There were a lot of angry parents.

Canada: They . . . they were angry and they were accusing me, "Geoff, how could you do this to a three-year-old? This is not right, Geoff." And I would say, "No, no, you're right, it's not right."

Woman 3: I was sitting here . . .

Canada: Yes.

Woman 3: . . . for nothing.

Canada: You look into those mothers' eyes and those fathers' eyes, and you see the fear and the terror and the clear understanding that the system is designed so that their kids are probably not going to make it if they don't get in. . . . (to audience) Who else?

Reporter: To help ensure that the kids who don't get in still make it to college, Canada has created a pipeline of free programs targeting all 10,000 children in the zone. He sends recruiters out door to door trying to sell sometimes suspicious families on what services he's offering.

Man 1: [knocks on door] You have a moment?

Woman 4: No.

Reporter: Canada's pipeline begins at birth, at the baby college, a nine-week workshop that teaches new mothers and fathers how to parent.

Woman 5: You know, you're hitting, and then, you know, after that you come and hug the child. It's sending mixed messages.

Reporter: It also teaches them how to prepare their kids for elementary school.

Woman 6: So you have the routine of reading books.

Reporter: For toddlers, there are free pre-kindergarten classes that focus on developing language skills, even in French and Spanish. . . . (children singing in French) . . . Canada's also put reading labs in public elementary schools in the zone and created an SAT tutoring center for teens.

Woman 7: You have to line it up to this one.

Reporter: Ninety percent of the zone's public high school students who participate in Canada's afterschool programs now go on to college.

Canada: We get them in the pipeline, we seal it. Once they get in, we don't let you out. You get out with a college degree. That's the point.

Reporter: None of this comes cheap, however. The Children's Zone annual budget is seventy-six million dollars [$76,000,000], two-thirds of which comes from the private sector, and much of that from Wall Street. It comes to about five thousand dollars [$5,000] per child per year. . . . (to Canada) Five thousand per kid. That's . . . it's a lot of money.

Canada: Yeah, it's a lot of money until you see what it cost us when we fail these kids. In New York City jail, sixty thousand dollars [$60,000] a year.

Reporter: Sixty?

Canada: Juvenile detention, a hundred thousand plus [≥$100,000] a year. We're spending the money on these kids, and we're not getting anything in return.

Reporter: Canada's long argued that investing in the Harlem Children's Zone would show a return, and now, for the first time, there's scientific data to prove it.

Dr. Fryer: He has done a remarkable job.

Reporter: Dr. [Doctor] Roland Fryer is a professor in the economics department at Harvard. He has conducted the first independent statistical study of Geoffrey Canada's efforts to close the racial achievement gap in his school. What is the racial achievement gap?

Dr. Fryer: Black children in our schools are not performing at even close the rate as white children in our schools. The average black 17-year-old reads at the proficiency level of the average white 13-year-old. A four-year difference in effective reading skills: that's . . . that's huge.

Reporter: But when Dr. Fryer analyzed four years' worth of Promise Academy test scores, he discovered something remarkable.

Dr. Fryer: At the elementary school level he closed the achievement gap in both subjects: math and reading.

Reporter: Actually eliminating the gap in elementary school?

Dr. Fryer: Absolutely. We've never seen . . . we've never seen anything like that. Absolutely eliminating the gap. The gap is gone, and that is absolutely incredible.

Reporter: Last year, according to New York State data, a hundred percent of Canada's third-graders scored at or above grade level in math . . .

Teacher 2: Good job.

Reporter: . . . narrowly outperforming their white peers in the city's public schools.

Teacher 3: Ninety-six. Is that the answer?

Students: Yes.

Reporter: Even more impressive, Canada's impact on middle schoolers: kids who enrolled in the Promise Academy in the sixth grade. They started out far behind grade level, but Dr. Fryer found that within three years they had virtually eliminated the achievement gap in math and reduced it by nearly half in reading.

Dr. Fryer: These are kids that a lot of people had given up on. And he showed that it's never too late.

Reporter: Does it change the way you look at the problem?

Dr. Fryer: It does, because here's an analogy. We're ten touchdowns down in the fourth quarter. We kick a field goal and everyone celebrates, right? (laughing) That's kind of useless. We . . . we're . . . we're still 67 points down.

Reporter: Still losing.

Dr. Fryer: OK. We're not just losing; we're getting crushed. All right? What Geoff Canada has shown is that we can actually win the game.

Reporter: Geoffrey Canada may be winning, but he's nowhere near declaring victory. Reversing the black-white achievement gap and then closing it in elementary school, that's . . . that's huge.

Canada: It . . . it's . . . it's about an hour's worth of celebration huge. You know I've got kids who might be shot tomorrow. We've still got a lot of work to do before I can feel comfortable that they're all going be OK.

Reporter: According to Canada, four kids in the Children's Zone were shot to death this past year; four others were wounded. . . . (to Canada) There . . . there's been an uptick in violence?

Canada: Yeah, there's been . . . there's been an uptick in violence.

Reporter: And the economic crisis has hit Canada hard as well: donations are down and he's laid off staff. His endowment also lost four million

dollars to Bernie Madoff. . . . (to Canada) And that money's just gone?

Canada: We basically have written that money off. It's basically gone.

Reporter: But Canada's experiment did receive a boost earlier this year when President Obama announced plans to create 20 Promise Neighborhoods across the country, modeled after the Harlem Children's Zone.

Pres. Obama: If the Harlem's Children's Zone can turn around neighborhoods in New York, then why not Detroit or San Antonio or Los Angeles?

Canada: And a lot of students came to school on Saturday.

Reporter: There are other charter schools getting similar positive results, but replicating the Harlem Children's Zone in its entirety may be difficult, in part because it's hard to determine exactly which ingredient is the key to Geoffrey Canada's success.

Dr. Fryer: I feel like I've gone to a phenomenal French restaurant. The dish tastes good, but I'm not sure exactly what they did to do it.

Reporter: He . . . he's doing so many different things. He's got this all-hands-on-deck approach.

Dr. Fryer: He does. He does. He does. And I think the . . . the key step forward from here is that we need to kind of demystify the success. I want to boil him down to pill form, so we can transport him to other places. Because if folks think, well, this is just Geoff Canada or this is just Harlem and this is just a special deal, they're less likely to adopt it in Omaha and places like Minnesota.

Canada: And we're going to stick with them through college, right?

Reporter: So, how will you measure success? How will you know when the Children's Zone has worked?

Canada: When I see my kids by the thousands with degrees. . . . (to students) Wow. Good job. . . . (interview) . . . I will say this is what we set out to do, and we've done it. We've got our kids in the best schools in America. They're going to be successful. They'll be competing with everybody else all over the country. People will be looking for kids from Harlem, saying, "Oh, those kids are so great from Harlem. We need more kids from Harlem to come in." Then, we'll be successful.